Finlayson, Bousfield

Rules and Directions for the Use of Finlayson, Bousfield &

Co.'s

Real Scotch Linen Crochet Thread

Finlayson, Bousfield

Rules and Directions for the Use of Finlayson, Bousfield & Co.'s
Real Scotch Linen Crochet Thread

ISBN/EAN: 9783337409241

Printed in Europe, USA, Canada, Australia, Japan

Cover: Foto ©Lupo / pixelio.de

More available books at **www.hansebooks.com**

RULES AND DIRECTIONS
for the use of

FINLAYSON, BOUSFIELD & CO'S

Real Scotch
Linen

Crochet Thread.

FINLAYSON BOUSFIELD & CO

RULES AND DIRECTIONS

––––––– FOR THE USE OF –––––––

FINLAYSON, BOUSFIELD & CO.'S

REAL SCOTCH

LINEN CROCHET THREAD.

Introductory Chapter.

AMONGST vegetable fibres adapted to the use of mankind in the fabrication of garments or coverings, and for ornamentation, flax occupies a conspicuous place, both in respect of extended application, and the antiquity of its use. The Phœnicians and the Egyptians were proficient in flax culture, as well as in linen manufacture; with them "purple and fine linen" were synonymous with refinement and wealth.

The skilful manipulation of the flax fibre was well understood and practised by the children of Israel. In Tyre and Sidon, as Isaiah tells us, "they work in fine flax, and weave net works." In all subsequent ages as history shows, flax has been grown, spun, and woven: it has been worn by priests, sages, and warriors for attire or adornment on occasions of honor or display. The maids of Athens, the fair dames of Rome, the bonnie lassies of Saxonland and Scandinavia, the beauties of France, have all been familiar with distaff and spindle; and through the long vista of the past have tuned their ditties to the merry whirl of the spinning-wheel. Show one of these homely implements to any New Englander past middle age, and a flood of eloquence will be unloosed. You will soon learn about the sister or the mother whose ready fingers deftly spun the smoothest yarn, from home-grown flax on the old farm, in the far off days when thrift ruled the household: wild strawberries tasted *like* strawberries then, and the speckled trout if anything, rather wanted to be caught by the boys, so it seemed.

Our farmers no longer grow their flax for home consumption, and the maidens have lost the art of spinning yarn; and yet flax holds its own in our homes; with netting, knitting, crochet, and outline work as vehicles for the display of its adaptability, it advances to still more artistic forms of service; and it requires not the eye of a prophet to foresee the continuous thread of its use extending through ages yet to come, in even more beautiful forms than any attained in the past.

> "And the whirling of a wheel
> Dull and drowsy makes me feel;
> Gleam the long threads in the sun,
> While within this brain of mine
> Cobwebs, brighter and more fine
> By the busy wheel are spun."

No more fascinating way of filling up the spare moments could be devised than in working out the designs herein given, or in the origination of new forms and fancies in crochet work, or in designing colored outlines upon felt or linen.

REAL SCOTCH CROCHET THREAD.

In order to knit or crochet well it is necessary to understand the terms used.

Knitting.

To CAST ON — make a loop in your thread, and place it on the needle in your left hand; when with your right-hand needle, knit this stitch; but, instead of letting off the first, place the second stitch on the same needle with the first. Repeat this till you have the required amount of stitches.

To MAKE A STITCH — is to bring the thread forward or put it over; if after a seamed stitch, turn thread quite around needle.

To NARROW — decrease by knitting two stitches together.

To SLIP A STITCH — pass it from one needle to the other without knitting it.

TWIST STITCH — like plain knitting, only the needle should be put in the back of the stitch, instead of front, after which knit as usual.

To SEAM — is to knit with the thread before the needle.

To BIND OFF — knit two plain stitches, pass first over the second, and so on to the last stitch, when draw thread through.

Crocheting.

To many this work seems quite difficult as they cannot understand the changes. Now we give an illustrated plate of stitches which appeared some years ago in the *Ladies' Floral Cabinet*, but is of great assistance to crocheters.

CHAIN-STITCH — is the foundation of all crochet. A loop is made on the hook, and through this the thread is drawn. A second loop being thus made, the thread is drawn through it; and so on, until chain is length required.

SLIP-STITCH. — A chain being made, the hook is inserted in the last stitch but one to that already on the needle, and the thread drawn through both together; then in the next stitch, and so on. This stitch is used to fasten off portions of crochet a good deal, rendering it firm and neat.

SINGLE CROCHET (*Sc*). — In this the thread is drawn through the chain of the last row, and forms a second loop on the needle. Through the two loops the thread is drawn at once.

DOUBLE CROCHET (*Dc*). — The thread is passed *once* over the needle, before the hook is inserted in the chain through which the thread is drawn; there will thus be *three* loops on the needle. Draw the thread through *two*, which leaves *one* and the *new loop*. Draw the thread through these; thus, by this completing the stitch.

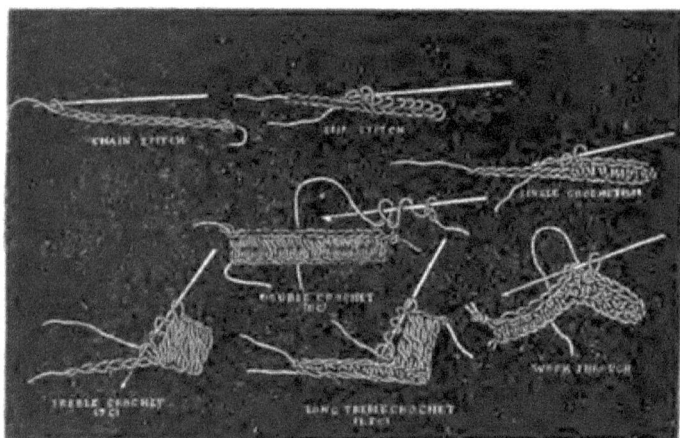

TREBLE CROCHET (*Tc*) is worked precisely like *Dc*; but the thread being put *twice* over the needle, instead of *once*, the stitch is completed by drawing the thread *three* times through two loops.

LONG TREBLE CROCHET (*Long Tc*). — Like *Tc.*, except that the thread is put *three* times around the needle, and drawn four successive times through two loops.

P, or PICOT — is made by chaining three stitches and making one *Sc.*, in first stitch of chain.

HALF TREBLE. — Turn the thread over the hook, pass the hook through a stitch of the foundation, draw through, turn thread again over hook, draw thread through all *three* loops at once

CROSS TREBLE. — *Turn the thread twice around the hook, insert the hook into a stitch, turn the thread over the hook, draw through the stitch, turn the thread over the hook, draw through two loops together, turn the thread over the hook, pass by two stitches, insert the hook into the next stitch, draw through, (pass thread over the hook, draw through two loops) twice, pass the thread over the hook, draw through all the loops on the hook together, two chain, one treble into centre of cross treble.* Repeat from * to *

Wide Crocheted Edge.

(See hints at end of Lace.)

MATERIALS. — Two or three balls of Finlayson, Bousfield & Co.'s, REAL SCOTCH LINEN CROCHET THREAD No. 70 or coarser if wished. Steel hook, pillow-shams, dresses, tidies, etc., look pretty trimmed with it.

Make a chain of 90 stitches. 1 A row — pass by 7 stitches, 1 treble crochet in 8th foundation chain, 2 chain, miss 2 chain, * 4 treble crochet in next 4 stitches, 8 chain, miss 8 stitches, 5 short crochet in the next 5 chain, 8 chain, miss 8 stitches, *. Repeat from * to * twice, 4 tc, in the last 4 stitches, turn work.

Second Row. — 15 chain, 3 tc, in the 3 first stitches of the 15 chain, 1 tc, in the next tc, * 2 chain, miss 2 stitches, 4 tc, in the next 4 stitches, 5 chain, miss 5 stitches, 5 short crochet in the next 5 short crochet stitches in last row, 5

chain, miss 5 stitches, 4 tc, in the next 4 stitches, * repeat from * to * twice, 2 chain, miss 2 stitches, 1 tc, in next stitch, miss 2 stitches, 1 tc, in the next tc, 2 chain, miss 2 stitches, 1 tc, in third stitch, turn.

Third Row. — 5 chain, 1 tc, in second tc, of last row, 3 more loops formed by 2 chain and 1 tc, 4 tc, in next chain stitch, * 4 chain, miss 4 stitches, 1 tc, in the centre of the 5 short crochet in last row, 4 chain, miss 4 stitches, 4 treble crochet in the next 4 stitches, 4 chain, 1 dc, in next loop, 4 chain, 1 treble crochet in the last of the next 4 treble crochet in last row, 3 tc, in the first 3 chain stitches of last row. *

Repeat from * to * twice.

Fourth Row. — 15 chain, 3 tc, in the first 3 chain stitches, 1 tc, in first tc, of last row * 5 chain, miss 5 stitches 5 short crochets in next 5 stitches, 5 chain, miss 5 stitches, 4 tc, in next 4 stitches, 2 chain, miss 3 stitches, 4 tc, in next 4 stitches. *

Repeat from * to * twice.

Fifth Row. — 6 chain, 4 tc, in the next 4 stitches, * 8 chain, miss 8 stitches, 5 short crochet in the next 5 short crochet, 8 chain, miss 8 stitches, 4 long crochet in the next 4 stitches. *

Repeat from * to * twice, make 5 loops.

Fifth Row. — 6 chain, 4 tc, in the next 4 stitches, * 8 chain, miss 8 stitches, 5 short crochet in next 5 short crochet, 8 chain, miss 8 stitches, 4 tc, in next 4 stitches.

Repeat from * to * twice.

Sixth Row. — 15 chain, 3 tc, in first 3 chain, 1 tc, in next tc, * 2 chain, miss 2 stitches, 4 tc, in next 4 stitches, 5 chain, miss 5 stitches, 5 short crochet in next 5 short crochet, 5 chain, miss 5 stitches, 4 tc, in next 4 stitches. *

Repeat from * to * twice, make 7 loops.

Seventh Row. — Chain 8, * 4 tc, in next 4 stitches, 4 chain, miss 4 stitches, 1 dc, in the centre of the 5 short crochet in last row, 4 chain, miss 4 stitches, 4 tc, in the next 4 stitches, 4 chain, miss 4 stitches, 1 dc, in next loop, 4 chain, miss 4 stitches. *

Repeat from * to * twice, 4 tc, in next 4 stitches.

Eighth Row — 15 chain, 4 tc, in next 4 stitches, * chain, miss 5 stitches, 5 short crochet in next 5 stitches, 5 chain, miss 5 stitches, 4 tc, in next 4 stitches, 2 chain, miss 3 stitches, 4 tc, in next 4 stitches. *

Repeat from * to * twice, 9 loops.

Ninth Row. — Chain 10, 4 tc, in next 4 stitches, * 8 chain, miss 8 stitches, 5 short crochet in the next 5 stitches, 8 chain, miss 8 stitches, 4 tc, in the next 4 stitches. *

Repeat from * to * twice.

Tenth Row. — 15 chain, 3 tc, in the first 3 chain, 1 tc, in next stitch, * 2 chain, miss 2 stitches, 4 tc, in next 4 stitches, 5 chain, miss 5 stitches, 5 short crochet in the 5 short crochet of last row, 5 chain, miss 5 stitches, 4 tc, in next 4 stitches. *

Repeat from * to * twice, 11 loops.

Eleventh Row. — 12 chain, 4 tc, in next 4 stitches, * 4 chain, miss 4 stitches,

1 dc, in centre stitch of the 5 short crochets in last row, 4 chain, miss 4 stitches, 4 tc, in the next 4 stitches, 4 chain, miss 4 stitches, 1 dc, in next loop, 4 chain, miss 4 stitches, 4 long crochet in next 4 stitches. *

Repeat from * to * twice.

Twelfth Row. — Chain 15, 3 tc, in first 3 chain stitches, 1 tc, in next stitch, * 5 chain, miss 5 stitches, 4 tc, in the next 4 stitches, 2 chain, miss 3 stitches, 4 tc, in the next 4 stitches. *

Repeat from * to * twice, 13 loops.

Thirteenth Row. — 14 loops, 4 tc, in the next 4 stitches, * 8 chain, miss 8 stitches, 5 short crochets in the 5 of last row, 8 chain, miss 8 stitches, 4 tc, in next 4 stitches. *

Repeat from * to * twice.

Fourteenth Row. — 11 chain, miss 3 stitches, 4 tc., in next 4 stitches of last row, * 5 chain, miss 5 stitches, 5 short crochet in the 5 short crochet of last row, 5 chain, miss 5 stitches, 4 tc, in next 4 stitches, 2 chain, miss 2 stitches, 4 tc, in next 4 stitches. *

Repeat from * to * twice, 13 loops.

Fifteenth Row.—12 loops, 4 tc, in next 4 stitches, * 4 chain, 1 dc, in next loop, 4 chain, miss 3 tc, of last row, 4 tc, in next 4 stitches, 4 chain, 1 dc, in centre stitch of the 5 short crochet in last row, 4 chain, miss 4 stitches, 4 tc, in next 4 stitches. *

Repeat from * to * twice.

Sixteenth Row. — 11 chain, miss 3 tc, 4 tc, in next 4 stitches, * 2 chain, miss 3 stitches, 4 tc, in next 4 stitches, 5 chain, miss 5 stitches, 5 short crochet in next 5 stitches, 5 chain, miss 5 stitches, 4 tc, in next 4. *

Repeat from * to * twice, 11 loops.

Seventeenth Row. — 10 loops, 4 tc, in next 4, * 8 chain, miss 8 stitches, 5 short crochet in the 5 of last row, 5 chain, miss 8 stitches, 4 tc, in next 4 stitches. *

Repeat from * to * twice.

Eighteenth Row. — 11 chain, miss 3 stitches, 4 tc, in next 4, * 5 chain, 5 short crochet in 5 of last row, 5 chain, miss 5 stitches, 4 tc, in next 4, 2 chain, miss 2 stitches, 4 tc, in next 4. *

Repeat from * to * twice, 9 loops.

Nineteenth Row.—8 loops, 4 tc, in next 4, * 4 chain, 1 dc, in next loop, 4 chain, miss 3 tc, 4 tc, in next 4, 4 chain, 1 tc, in centre stitch of the 5 in last row, 4 chain, miss 4, 4 tc, in next 4. *

Repeat from * to * twice.

Twentieth Row. — 11 chain, miss 3 stitches, 4 tc, crochet in next 4, * 2 chain, miss 3 stitches, 4 tc, in next 4, 5 chain, miss 5 stitches, 5 short crochet in next 5, 5 chain, miss 5 stitches, 4 tc, in next 4. *

Repeat from * to * twice, 7 loops,

Twenty-first Row. — 6 chain, 4 tc, in next 4, * 8 chain, miss 8 stitches, 5 short crochets in 5 of last row, 8 chain, miss 8 stitches, 4 tc. in next 4 stitches. *

Repeat from * to * twice.

Twenty-second Row. — 11 chain, miss 3 stitches, 4 tc, in next 4, * 5 chain, miss 5 stitches, 5 short crochet in 5 of last row, 5 chain, miss 5 stitches, 4 tc, in next 4, 2 chain, miss 2 stitches, 4 tc, in next 4. *

Repeat from * to * twice, 5 loops.

Twenty-third Row. — 4 loops, 4 tc, in next 4, * 4 chain, 1 dc, in next loop, 4 chain, miss the 3 tc, in last row, 4 tc, in next 4, 4 chain, 1 dc, in centre of 5 of last row, 4 chain, miss 4 stitches, 4 tc, in next 4. *

Repeat from * to * twice.

Twenty-fourth Row. — 11 chain, miss 3 stitches of last row, 4 tc, in next 4, * 2 chain, miss 3 stitches, 4 tc, in next 4, 5 chain, miss 5 stitches, 5 short crochet in next 5, 5 chain, miss 5 stitches, 4 tc, in next 4. *

Repeat from * to * twice, 3 loops.

You have now become familiar enough with the pattern to do the insertion without directions.

With same materials make a chain of 91 stitches.

This work may be done narrower, both lace and insertion, by chaining a less number at beginning.

To do dc in this lace or insertion, instead of drawing through two loops at a time draw through all 3 at once. To do the tc, of this put thread over once, insert, draw thread through 2 stitches, then through last 2.

Vandyke Crocheted Lace.

Same materials as before. Make a foundation chain length required, into which work 1 chain, 1 dc, into every 2nd stitch.

Second Row. — * 5 chain, 2 tc, missing 3 chain. *

Repeat from * to *.

Third Row. — 1 chain, 1 dc, into every other stitch and fasten off.

Make half stars separately, work a 14 chain, form a round, and surround it with slip stitch; into the upper half of round work 7 loops, putting them into the stitches one after the other. The first loop requires 24 chain, second and third 16 each, middle loop 24, repeat first 3 loops reversing their order; unite the plain part of the round to the border, crocheting them together, and fasten the stars at a distance of 48 stitches from each other.

Fourth Row. — Commence at 22nd stitch from centre of star, * work 3 chain, and pick up 1st loop 6 chain, pick up second loop 6 chain, pick up 3d loop 8 chain, pick up middle loop, repeat backwards for 3 loops, and fasten into 22nd stitch from the middle of the star, slip cotton along 4 stitches. *

Repeat from * to *.

5th Row. — Work a dc into every chain except the one in the centre loop, in this one the increase is managed and requires 1 dc, 2 chain, 1 dc, for the lattice part work 4 chain, catch it into 3d row, and then 4 chain.

Repeat 5th row eleven times, always increasing at the pointed stitch, and for the lattice part work a plain 8 chain alternately with 4 chain caught into 3d stitch of previous row and 4 chain. Work the border from illustration.

Beautiful Edge, Crocheted.

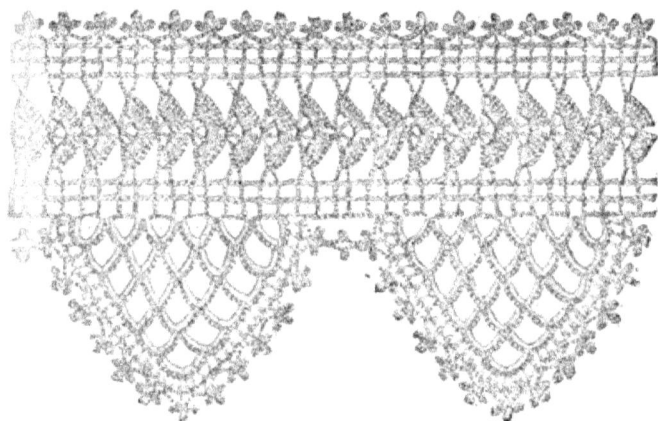

Of the same thread as previously described, do the insertion part first by making a chain of 23 stitches. Work the insertion like design until it is length required, then add the heading and bottom finish. When No. 17 REAL SCOTCH CROCHET THREAD and coarse steel hook is used, a pretty lambrequin may be made of this design. Add tassels between points.

Another Wide Edge.

Of same materials given before. Do the insertion part commencing with a chain of 53 stitches, when you have a piece long enough, crochet the two rows on bottom for a finish.

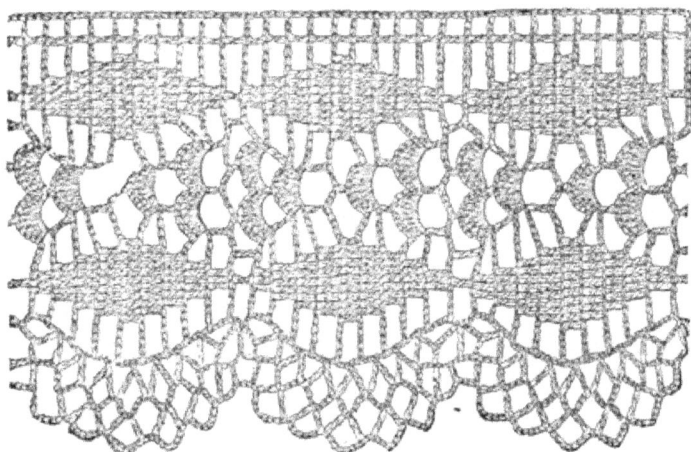

Another Wide Edge. See description on page 10.

Insertion. See description on page 12.

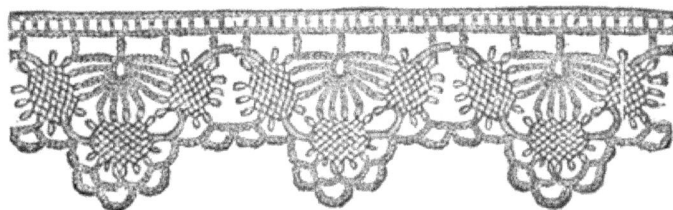

Fancy Braid Edge. See description on page 12.

Crocheted Fancy Braid and Insertion.

MATERIALS — fancy braid which comes by the piece, and Finlayson, Bousfield & Co.'s, REAL SCOTCH CROCHET THREAD. The pattern is easily worked from design.

Medallion Lace.

MATERIALS. — Finlayson, Bousfield & Co.'s, No. 70 REAL SCOTCH CROCHET THREAD, or courser if wished

Medallion lace for dress trimming :—It may be used in a variety of ways—for trimming children's dresses and cloaks, overdresses, aprons; whole fronts of dresses may be made of these medallions.

Directions for making one medallion :—Make a chain of 10 stitches; join in a circle.

1st round.—22 short crochets in circle ; fasten together with a single crochet on the first short crochet.

2d round.—4 chain, 21 long crochets, with 1 chain between the stitches of last row, 1 chain, 1 single crochet in the third chain of beginning.

3d round.—* 1 picot formed by 5 chain, fasten back in first chain, 1 short crochet in next long crochet of last row ; * repeat from * to * 20 times, 1 picot, 1 single crochet in last stitch.   These 3 rounds finish 1 medallion ; join medallion as seen in cut.

The little figure is made as follows :—5 chain, fasten with a single crochet in first medallion, 4 chain, 1 single crochet in first chain, * 4 chain, fasten on next

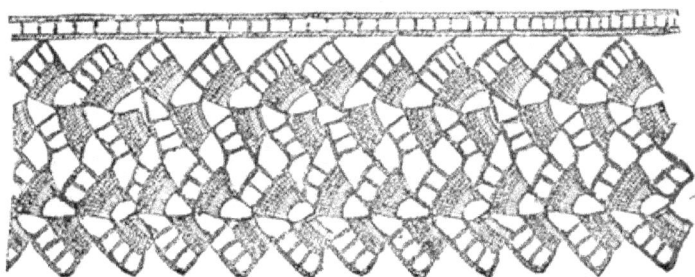

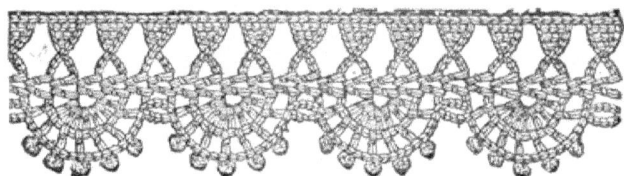

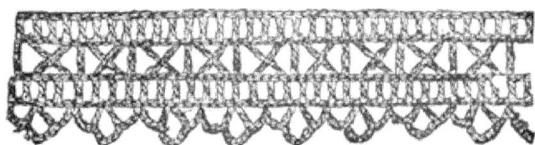

medallion, 4 chain, one single crochet in the first of 5 chain; * repeat from * to * twice; on top of medallion make * 5 chain, fasten on the third picot from the centre, 4 chain, fasten on the first of the 5 chain, 8 chain, miss 2 picots, 1 long crochet in next picot, 14 chain, miss 2 picots, fasten on the third picot, 4 chain, fasten back on the eleventh chain*; repeat from last * to * the last row, 1 long crochet, 1 chain, miss 1 stitch; continue to end of row This edging can be made any depth; the finish at top easily done from design.

By using heading and top row of medallions you have a pretty collar, then with 3 or 4 rows cuffs may be formed.

Crocheted Tidy.
(Boston Globe June 20.)

MATERIALS. — Finlayson, Bousfield & Co.'s, REAL SCOTCH CROCHET THREAD, about 2 balls No. 60 or coarser if wished. Steel crochet hook.

Begin at the middle rosette, which is worked in the following manner :—Close a foundation of twelve st (stitches) in a ring with one sl (slip stitch), and on this ring crochet the first round. Six times alternately, five ch (chain stitch), one sc (single crochet) on the second following foundation stitch.

2d round.—On each chain stitch scallop of the preceding round one sc, one s dc (short double crochet), five dc (double crochet), one sdc, one sc.

3d round.—One sc on each sc of the round before the last (the first, round passing the needle around the vertical veins of this round on the under side of the work), 6 ch, after each sc.

4th round.—Like the second, but work always 7 dc on the ch scallops instead of the five dc referred to in the second round.

5th round.—Like the third, but instead of the six ch given there, always work seven ch.

6th round.—Like the second, but work nine dc instead of five dc. Enlarge each ch scallop of the seventh round again by one st.

8th round.——Increase the dc of each scallop by two dc.

For the remainder these two rounds are worked in the following manner:—

9th round.—Always alternately one ch, one dc on the two upper veins of each second following st of the eighth round ; instead of the first ch at the beginning of the round, work four ch ; the first three of these count as one dc; at the end of the round fasten to the third of the three ch, counting as one dc with one st.

10th round.—Always alternately three ch, one sc, on the next ch of the preceding round.

11th round.—At the beginning of this round work sl to the middle of the next ch scallop, then always alternately three ch, one sc on the middle stitch of the following ch scallop of the preceding round.

12th and 17th rounds.—One sc on each ch scallop of the preceding round, five ch after each sc.

18th and 21st rounds.—One sc on each ch scallop of the preceding round, seven ch after each sc.

Surround the cover thus completed with small crocheted rosettes, which are worked, each separately, similar to the middle rosette of the part completed. Begin each rosette with a foundation of ten st, close these in a ring with one sl, and then work the first round. Five times alternately three ch, one sc on the second following foundation st. Then the second round. On each ch scallop of the preceding round work one sc, one s dc, three dc, one s dc, one sc.

Work two more leaflet circles in the same manner ; in the first round of the first of these two circles, work five ch for each leaflet; in the following round work on each five ch one sc, one s dc, five dc, one s dc, one sc; enlarge the leaflet of the third circle in the same proportion.

7th round.—On each leaflet of the sixth round work 5 dc, 1 ch after each dc; work 3 ch, instead of the first dc. At the end of the round fasten to the third of the 3 ch with 1 sl.

8th round.—Always alternately 1 sc on the next ch of the preceding round, 5 ch. In working this round fasten the rosettes to each other with 1 sl each, and to the completed centre of the cover also.

Work 5 rounds of alternating ch scallops, on the outer edge of the rosette circle thus joined, with the completed centre; each of the scallops counts 7 ch and 1 sc on the middle stitch of a ch scallop of the preceding round.

6th round.—Work 2 dc divided by 3 ch on the same ch scallop on which the last sc of the preceding round has been worked (in this, as well as in the following rounds, work 3 ch instead of the first dc)* 3 ch, 5 dc on the following ch scallop, of the preceding round, 3 ch, 2 dc, divided by 3 ch on the following ch scallop, and repeat from *. At the end of this, as well as of each of the following rounds, fasten to the third of the 3 ch that count as first dc of the round with 1 sl, and work 1 sl to the middle of the following ch scallop.

7th round.—Two dc divided by three ch, on the 1st ch scallop (this is the same scallop on the first stitches of which sl has been worked), * four ch 10 dc (these are worked on the one ch before the next five dc of the preceding round, on the following five dc and the one ch after the five dc referred to), working always two dc on each of the two ch and on the middle dc of the five dc, 4 ch two dc divided by three ch on the ch scallop between the next two dc of the preceding round, and repeat from *.

8th round.—* Two dc divided by four ch on the ch scallop between the next two dc of the preceding round, five ch eight dc on the middle eight dc of the next 10 dc of the preceding round, five ch, and repeat from *.

9th round.—* Two dc divided by four ch on the ch scallops between the next two dc of the preceding round, six ch six dc on the six middle dc of the 8 dc of the preceding round, six ch, and repeat from *.

10th round.—* dc divided by five ch on the ch, scallop between the next two dc of the preceding round, seven ch four dc on the middle four dc of the next six dc of the preceding round seven ch and repeat from *.

11th round.—* 2 dc divided by 8 ch on the ch scallop between the next 2 dc of the preceding round, 8 ch 2 dc on the two middle dc of the next 4 dc of the preceding round, 8 ch, and repeat from *.

12th round.—* 2 dc divided by 9 ch on the ch scallop between the next 2 dc of the preceding round, 9 ch 1 dc on the next 2 dc of the preceding round, (to do this, pass the needle through the two upper veins which meet of both stitches, so that the 1 dc of the 12th round comes on the middle of the 2 dc referred to,) 9 ch, and repeat from * till size required.

Wheel Tidy, Crocheted.

MATERIALS.—Finlayson, Bousfield & Co.'s, No. 50, or finer, REAL SCOTCH CROCHET THREAD, steel hook.

Nineteen wheels are made for tidy then fastened together, and the tidy finished all round with an edging, (see design.)

Section of Wheel Tidy.

For one rosette or wheel, chain 5 stitches and close into a ring.

1st round.—Work 6 treble crochet each separated by 3 chain.

2nd round.—* 5 double trebles under 3 chain, 3 chain, * repeat from * to * 5 times more.

3rd round.—* 5 double trebles under 3 chain, 9 chain, * repeat from * to * 5 times more.

4th round.—* 1 double treble into each of 5 double trebles of last round, 4 chain, 1 double treble into the 5th of 9 chain, 4 chain, * repeat from * to * 5 times more.

When all the rosettes or wheels are joined together put on edge, all round tidy.

1st row.—1 double crochet into each stitch.

2nd and 3rd rows.—Cross trebles separated by 3 chain, (cross treble is described among terms for crochet.)

4th row.—* 1 double into a stitch, 4 chain, 1 double into the first, pass by 1 stitch * repeat from * to * to end of row.

Lastly finish edge all round with little picots of 3 chain.

Imported German Tidy, Crocheted.

MATERIALS.—2 balls No. 70, Finlayson, Bousfield & Co.'s, REAL SCOTCH CROCHET THREAD, fine steel hook.

Examine design closely and it will be seen that 25 large rosettes are first made separately then joined together with 4 smaller ones on every other row.

Crochet the border lastly.

We shall now proceed to give rules for some pretty rosettes which may be put together the same as this tidy.

Crocheted Wheel for Tidy No. 1.

Commence in centre with 8 chain, join round.

1st round.—16 double crochet under chain.

2nd round.—2 dc, into each stitch of last round.

3rd round.—*1 tc, into a stitch, 2 chain, pass by 1 stitch, * repeat from * to * all round.

4th round.—* 1 dc, into a stitch, 9 chain, work down the chain with 1 dc, 1 half treble, and 7 trebles, pass by 2 stitches of last round, 1 dc, into the next, 2 chain, pass by 2 stitches * repeat from * to * 7 times more.

5th round.—* 1 dc, over 2 chain of last round into 2 chain of 3rd round, then work up the 9 chain with 7 trebles, 1 half treble and 1 dc, 1 single crochet into the back horizontal loop of the half trebles and trebles first worked into the 9 chain, * repeat from * to * 7 times more. Work another row of leaves at the back of those already described in same way.

6th round.—* 1 dc, into point of leaf (see design) 6 chain, * repeat from * to * all round.

7th round.—* 1 tc, into a stitch, 2 chain, pass by 1 stitch * repeat from * to * all round.

8th round.—* 2 tc, separated by 3 chain into 1 stitch, 3 chain, pass by 4 stitches, * repeat from * to * all round.

9th round.—** 1 dc, into centre of 3 chain, 3 chain, 1 tc, into centre of 3 chain between the 2 trebles, * 4 chain, 1 dc, into first * repeat from * to * twice more, 1 dc, into top of tc, 3 chain, ** repeat from ** to **.

Wheel for Tidy No. 2.

Commence with chain of 16 stitches, join round.

1st round.—4 chain to take the place of a double treble, * 2 chain, 1 double treble under the 16 chain, * repeat from * to * 14 times more, 2 chain, join to top of first 4 chain with 1 single crochet.

2nd round.—4 dc, under each 2 chain of last round.

3rd round.—* 1 double treble into each of 3 stitches of last round, 4 chain, pass by 1 stitch * and repeat from * to * 15 times more.

4th round.—9 doubles under 4 chain, 3 doubles under next 4 chain, 11 chain, turn back and work 1 double into the 7th of 9 doubles, work 1 double into each of 11 chain except the 6th stitch, in this work 3 doubles, 6 doubles under same 4 chain the 3 doubles were worked into, turn, and work 1 chain, 1 treble into second of 13 doubles, 2 chain, 1 double treble into next stitch, 3 chain, 1 double treble into next stitch, * 3 chain, 1 triple treble into next stitch; * repeat from * to * 4 times more, 3 chain, 1 double treble into next stitch, 2 chain, 1 double treble into next stitch, 2 chain, 1 treble into next stitch, 1 chain, 1 dc, into first of 9 dc, 4 chain, 1 dc, under 2 chain, 4 chain, 1 dc, under 3 chain, ** 5 chain 1 dc, under 3 chain, ** repeat from ** to ** 6 times more, 4 chain, 1 dc, under 2 chain, 4 chain, 1 dc, into last of 9 dc, repeat from beginning of round.

Wheel for Tidy No. 3.

Commence in the centre with 8 chain, join round.

1st round.—1 double into a stitch, 3 into the next. Repeat from the beginning of the round 3 times more.

2nd to 4th rounds.—1 double into each stitch except at the corners; in these work 3 stitches.

5th round.—1 double into each of 5 stitches, 7 chain, pass over 3 stitches, 1 double into each of 5 stitches, 3 doubles into the next. Repeat from the beginning of the round 3 times more.

6th round.—1 double into each of 4 doubles, 7 chain, 1 double into the centre of 7 chain, 7 chain, 1 double into each of next 4 doubles, 3 doubles into the next. Repeat from the beginning of the row.

7th round.—1 double into each of 4 stitches, 7 chain, 1 double into centre of 7 chain of last round, 7 chain, 1 double into centre of next 7 chain, 7 chain, pass over 1 double, 1 double into each of 4 next stitches, and 3 into the next. Repeat from the beginning of the round 3 times more.

8th round.—1 double into each of 4 doubles, * 7 chain, 1 double into centre of 7 chain, repeat from * twice more, 7 chain, pass over 1 double, 1 double into each of 4 next doubles, and 3 into the next. Repeat from the beginning of the round 3 times more. Break off the cotton and fasten it at the back of the work.

9th round.—1 treble into centre of 9 doubles, * 5 chain, 1 treble into centre of 7 chain, repeat from * 3 times more, 5 chain. Repeat from the beginning of the round 3 times more.

10th round.—1 treble into a stitch, 2 chain, pass over 1 stitch, and repeat all round.

11th round.—1 double into a stitch, 11 chain, pass over 8 stitches, and repeat all round.

12th round.—1 double into the second, third, fourth, and fifth of 11 chain, 3 into the next, 1 into each of the 4 next stitches. Repeat from the beginning of the round.

13th round.—1 double between 2 vandykes of last round, 4 chain, 2 trebles separated by 5 chain into point of vandyke, 4 chain. Repeat from the beginning of the round.

14th round.—1 double into the second of 4 chain, 1 double into each of the 5 next stitches, 3 doubles into the next, and 1 into each of the 7 next stitches. Repeat from the beginning of the round.

Joining Star.

This is used to join wheels No. 9. 1, 2, 3 or any other.

Commence in the centre with sixteen chain, join round.

1st round.—1 double into a stitch, 5 chain, pass over 1 stitch, and repeat all round.

2nd round.—1 double into centre of 5 chain, 7 chain. Repeat all round.

3rd round.—1 double into centre of 7 chain, 7 chain. Repeat all round.

4th round.—1 double into double of last round, 3 chain, 2 trebles separated by three chain into centre of 7 chain, 3 chain. Repeat.

Crocheted Stripe for Tidy.

This is done from design easily by good crocheters. Make the rounds separately, join as seen in design, then add side edges last. Use the white or drab Finlayson, Bousfield & Co.'s, REAL SCOTCH CROCHET THREAD, about No. 60. This may be worked over a fine cotton cord to make it firm. Make as many strips as necessary, join and trim top and bottom with knotted fringe of the thread, or the stripes may be used with velvet or satin.

Child's Collar, Crocheted.

Use about No. 50 or 60 REAL SCOTCH CROCHET THREAD. Make a chain of 378 stitches, and work in rows.

First Row.— Pass by first 3 stitches, 1 dc, on every following stitch.

Second Row.— Turn, chain 10, pass 7, * 2 dc, separated by 3 chain, on the following 2, 7 chain, pass by 6, 1 dc, on the next, 7 chain, pass by 6. *   Repeat from * to *, but in the last pattern of the row omit the chain after the last double, in the following rounds also, as well as in this.

Third Row. — Turn, chain 8, * 6 dc, around the next 3 chain between 2 dc, 5 chain, 1 dc, on the following 2nd dc, 5 chain. *   Repeat from * to *.

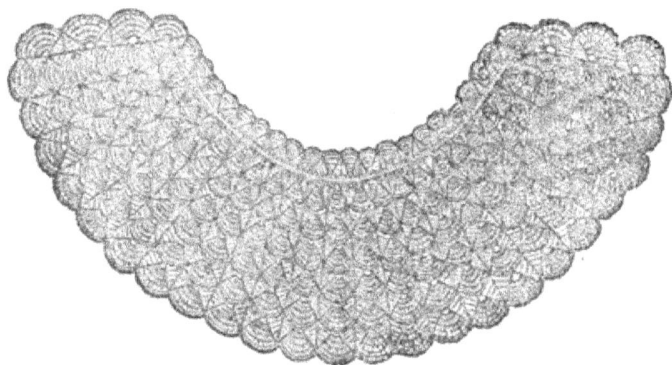

Fourth Row. — Turn, 7 chain, * 6 dc, separated by 1 chain, on the next 6 dc, 4 chain, 1 dc, on the following dc, 4 chain. *   Repeat from * to*.

Fifth Row. — Turn, 6 chain, * 5 dc, separated by 2 chain, around the chain between the 6 dc, in last row, 3 chain, 1 dc, on the following second dc, 3 chain. * Repeat from * to *.

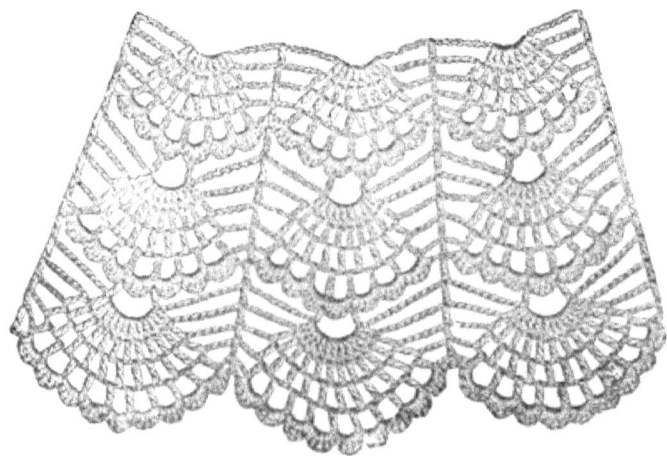

Section of Above Collar.

Sixth Row.—5 chain, * 3 times by turns 1 dc, around the next 2 chain between 2 dc, and 3 chain, then 1 dc, around the following 2 chain, 2 chain, 1 dc, on the following second dc, 2 chain *. Repeat from * to *.

Seventh Row.—2 chain, * 3 times a scallop composed of 1 single crochet, 3 dc, and 1 single crochet around the next 3 chain, then 1 chain, 1 dc, on the following second double, 1 chain *. Repeat from * to *.

Following this pattern there are 4 repetitions of it, in each of which the shell is slightly larger than in the preceding one. To accomplish this, work the 2 dc, separated by 3 chain of first row on both sides of the middle scallop in the preceding row in the next 3 repetitions, and in the fourth work them on the middle double of the middle 2 scallops; work 1 chain more between these 2 dc, in every repetition, and in the fourth work 8 chain on both sides instead of 7; in the second row of the first 3 repetitions work 8 dc, instead of 6, and in the fourth work 10 dc, which will cause a corresponding increase in the following rows and in the scallops in the last. Lastly surround the entire collar with an edging in same pattern, increasing at corners as needed.—*Harper's Bazaar.*

Baby's Bonnet, Crocheted.

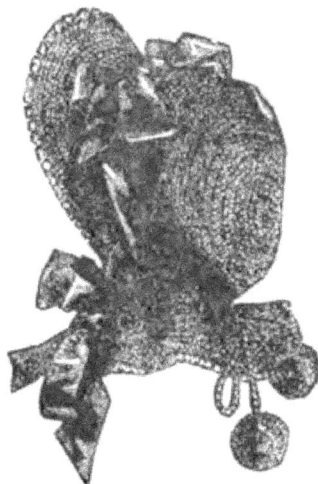

Three balls coarsest number of Finlayson, Bousfield & Co.'s, REAL SCOTCH CROCHET THREAD, 3 yards of ribbon, color of satin, lining 2 inches wide.

Commence in the centre of the crown with 4 stitches, join round; work 12 double under the chain over a fine cotton cord; this will give firmness to the work, and dispense with the necessity for a stiff shape; increase gradually in every round by working two stitches in every fourth stitch, until the crown is the size required   In the next row pass over every fifth stitch, doubles into the rest. Work one inch without increase or decrease. Now work in rows backwards and forwards, leaving a third of the band unworked for the opening for the neck.

For the brim, work on one-third of the centre-stitches in front of the band at the end of each row work on three more stitches of the last row of the head, and increase three times in each alternate row to raise the front of the bonnet ; this increase must be made about six times   Continue until you have worked up the last stitches of the band

The curtain is best soft, therefore should not be worked over the cord. Work quite across the back or bonnet, commencing at the brim on one side, and finishing at the brim on the other side. Sew a wire to the edge of the brim : line with satin, leaving it full at the edge to form a little puffing ; run a cord through the back above the curtain, tie in a bow, and finish the ends with balls. The ribbon is arranged in bows at the top, and is twisted and brought down each side, where it is sewn, and ends are left to form strings.

Child's Collar.

MATERIALS. — 2 pieces medallion braid, 2 balls Finlayson, Bousfield & Co.'s, REAL SCOTCH CROCHET THREAD No. 70 white.

This collar is worked in crochet on a foundation of medallion braid with medium fine cotton. Take an end of braid about twenty inches long, and work on it as follows:

1st round. — 1 leaflet, consisting of 3 tc (treble crochet), the uppermost veins of which are worked off together, in the first loop on the next medallion, 3 times alternately 5 ch (chain stitch) and 1 leaflet like the preceding one in the next loop, then 5 ch, 1 leaflet in the following second loop, * 1 leaflet in the first loop on the next medallion, 5 ch, 2 leaflets separated by 5 ch in the middle 2 loops on the same medallion, 5 ch, 1 leaflet in the last loop on the same medallion; repeat from * up to one medallion from the end, then on the last medallion work in inverse order as on the first; work 2 leaflets separated by 5 ch on the end of the braid, 5 ch, then repeat from the beginning of the round along the opposite side of the braid, and finish with 1 sl (slip stitch) on the first leaflet.

2nd round.—4 sl on the next 4 st (stitch) in the preceding round, 4 ch, of which the first 3 are considered as first dc (double crochet), 1 dc on the following 2d st, 5 times alternately 1 ch and 1 dc on the following 2d st, then 7 ch, pass 11 st, * 1 dc on the next st., 5 times alternately 1 ch and 1 dc on the following 2d st, then 7 ch, pass 9 st; repeat from * up to the last medallion, but in the last repetition pass 11 st instead of 9, after which work 1 dc on the next st, 6 times alternately 1 ch and 1 dc on the following 2d st, 6 ch, 3 times alternately 1 leaflet, composed of 3 qc (quadruple crochet), of which the uppermost veins are worked off together, around the next 5 ch, and 5 ch, then 2 leaflets separated by 5 ch around the following 6 ch, 5 ch, 3 leaflets separated by 5 ch around the next ch, twice alternately 5 ch and 1 leaflet around the next 6 ch, + 1 leaflet around the following 6 ch, 5 ch, 3 leaflets separated by 5 ch around the next 6 ch, 5 ch, 1 leaflet around the following 6 ch, repeat from + up to the opposite corner, where repeat in inverse order the work on the first; finish the round with 3 ch and 1 tc on the 3d of the 4 ch at the beginning.

3d round.—4 ch, 1 dc around the middle vein of the tc, 1 ch, 1 dc on the same st with the last tc in the preceding round, then alternately 1 dc in the following 2d st and 1 ch to the 5th of the 7 ch before the first leaflet in the preceding round; 9 times alternately 3 p (picot, consisting of 5 ch and 1 sc on the first of them) and 1 leaflet composed of qc around the next 5 ch, then * 2 p, twice 1 leaflet composed of tc around the next 5 ch, 2 p, 1 leaflet composed of qc around the following 5 ch, 3 p, 1 leaflet composed of qc on the next leaflet, 3 p, 1 leaflet composed of qc around the following 5 ch; repeat from * to the next corner, which work like the first; cut and fasten the thread; work the 4th–8th rounds along the top of the collar only.

4th round.—* 9 ch, 3 sc, of which the first 2 are separated by 7 ch and the last 2 by 5 ch, on the 5th of the 9 ch, thus forming 3 p, connecting the middle ch of the 7 to the second dc before the 1st leaflet in the preceding round; during this part of the work hold the collar with the lower edge turned upward; repeat from *, but at every repetition connect to the following 6th st.

5th round.—In connection with the preceding round, and working back over the st in that round, 5 ch, 1 sl on the first of them, * 4 sc, the 1st and 2d, and the 3d and the 4th, separated by 5 ch, and the middle 2 by 7 ch, on that st on which the next 3 sc in the preceding round were worked, 1 sl on the first of the next free 4 ch, 2 ch, 1 sl on the following 3d st, repeat from *, then 2 ch, 1 sl on the middle st of the first p in the preceding round, 2 ch, 1 sc on the st first connected to in the preceding round; cut and fasten the thread.

7th round.—Alternately 1 dc on the following 2d st in the preceding round and 1 ch.

8th round.—1 sl on the last leaflet in the 3d round, 3 p, 1 leaflet around the first 3 ch in the 6th round, 3 p, 1 leaflet around the next 8 ch, 3 p, 2 leaflets separated by 3 p around the next ch then alternately 3 p and 1 leaflet around the following 4th ch ; close by working in inverse order as at the beginning of the round.

Another Child's Collar, Crocheted.

Use feather-edge braid and Finlayson, Bousfield & Co.'s, REAL SCOTCH CROCHET THREAD, white. The lower part of the collar is filled in with small flowers and the wrong side of the work forms the right side of the collar. The rows or strips run up and down from the neck; three flowers in the first row alternating with two in the second. This model is given in size for a child of ten years.

Make 1 sc in the third loop from end of braid ; (a) 5 ch, miss 3 loops on the braid, 1 sc in the next loop ; repeat from (a) 4 times ; 11 ch miss 3 loops on braid, 1 sc in the next loop. (b) Turn the work or braid over and make the leaf on the other side, thus : 1 sc in the 1st stitch of the 11 ch counting from the stitch already on the needle ; 1 treble in each of the next 4 stitches, 1 sc in the next or 5th stitch. This forms the first leaf of the first flower. (There are three flowers in this row or strip of 6 leaves each.) Now, 5 ch, miss 3 loops on the braid, 1 sc in the next loop ; turn, work back on the 5 ch and make a leaf the same as the first leaf. In working up this side of the braid only two leaves of each flower are made, (except the third flower at the bottom of the row where all the leaves are made.) In working the opposite side of the braid the remaining 4 leaves are made.

Now go on with the work between the flowers thus : 7 ch, miss 3 loops on the braid, 1 sc in the next loop, 5 ch, miss 3 loops, 1 sc in next loop ; 5 ch, miss 3 loops, 1 sc in the next loop ; 11 ch, repeat from (b) once. The last stitch of each leaf is worked in the fifth stitch of the 11 ch which forms a small ring for the centre of flower.

Proceed to make the flower at the bottom of row which forms a scallop : 11 ch, miss 3 loops on braid, 1 sc in the next loop ; turn ; make a leaf the same as first leaf ; 5 ch, miss 3 loops on braid, 1 sc in the next loop : turn ; make a leaf the same as before. This forms the two leaves : (In working the remaining four leaves of this flower and the four leaves of each of the two succeeding flowers, do not turn the work.) Now for the third leaf : (c) 5 ch, miss 3 loops on braid, 1 sc in the next loop : turn, work back on the 5 ch and make the leaf, but remember not to turn the work over, on the wrong side; repeat from (c) 3 times.

The 6th leaf of each flower in all the rows is formed by working a treble in each of the five stitches left of the 11 ch, in beginning each flower; (d) 2 ch, 1 sc in the following loop on braid; 2 ch, 1 sc in the third loop of the 5 ch on opposite side; 2 ch, miss 3 loops on braid, 1 sc in the next loop; 2 ch, 1 sc in the 3d loop of the 5 ch; 1 ch, miss 3 loops, 1 sc in the next loop; 2 ch, miss 2 stitches of the 7 ch, 1 sc in the next stitch, 1 treble in each of the next stitches of 7 ch; (this forms the third leaf of second flower; the other three leaves are made the same as the last three leaves of the preceding flower;) repeat from (d) once; 2 ch, 1 sc in the following loop; (e) 2 ch, 1 sc in the third of the 5 ch on opposite side; 2 ch, miss 3 loops, 1 sc in the next loop; repeat from (e) 3 times; 5 ch, miss 3 loops on braid, 1 sc in each of the next 3 loops on braid.

This completes the first row or strip for the width and forms a scallop (there are 26 scallops in all) for the bottom of collar. Work 25 more strips in the same manner, repeating from the 5 chain, joining each scallop together as you continue the work. Fasten off securely and join the cotton to the first loop on the unworked side of the braid of this strip, and make a chain of (f) 3 stitches, miss 1 loop on braid, 1 sc in the next loop; repeat from (f) 39 times.

You now have reached the first inside row. Proceed to work as follows: 11 ch, miss 3 loops on braid, 1 sc in the next loop; turn the work and make the flower. There are two flowers in each of the inside rows, and the flowers are all made the same throughout the collar. The inside rows are made the same as the former rows of the collar, except after working the second flower of each row there are 8 spaces of 5 ch each. In making the 8 spaces do not miss the 3 loops on braid, but work 1 sc in each of the 7 successive loops. This turns the point for top of collar. Work up the other half of strip and around the scallops at the bottom of the next strip already made (which will bring you to second inside strip) thus: 2 ch, miss 1 loop on braid, 1 sc in the next loop; repeat 8 times.

Now go on and fill in the collar, working as in the above strip.

For the foundation edge around the neck of collar, fasten thread at the top of 1st strip and make 5 ch, 1 treble under the 1st 5 ch in beginning the strip, (*) 2 ch, 1 treble under the next 5 ch at the top of next strip, 2 ch, repeat from (*) all across; turn.

2d foundation row: 5 ch, 1 treble under the 1st 2 ch of previous row, (*) 2 ch, 1 treble under the next 2 ch, repeat from (*) to end.

For a finish around the neck, take another piece of braid and make a small strip of one flower each, thus: fasten thread in the 1st loop of braid and make (*) 5 ch, miss 3 loops, 1 sc in the next loop; 11 ch, miss 3 loops on braid, 1 sc in the next loop; turn. Go on and make the flower. After finishing the flower, make 2 ch, 1 sc in the following loop on braid; 2 ch, 1 sc in the 3d loop of the 5 ch on opposite side; 5 ch, miss 3 loops, 1 sc in each of the next 3 suc-

cessive loops. This forms a scallop; make 16 more scallops, repeating from
(*). Turn, make an edge around the scallops and fill in the strip on the unworked side of braid, thus: 3 ch, miss 1 loop on braid, (*) 1 sc in the next loop;
repeat from (*) 11 times, 5 ch, miss 3 loops, 1 sc in each of the next 8 loops on
braid; 2 ch, 1 sc in the 3d of the 5 ch on opposite side; 2 ch, miss 3 loops, 1
sc in the next loop; 3 ch, miss 1 loop, repeat from (*) to end.

This finishes the strip; dc it on around the neck so that it lies down over the
collar.

Pretty House Apron.

This apron is made of linen any shade desired, and ornamented with em-

broidered bands done with Finlayson, Bousfield & Co.'s embroidery floss, and
the crocheting done with their REAL SCOTCH CROCHET THREAD No.
60 or 70, or coarser.

To embroider the bands baste on piece of canvas over which the work is done than draw out the threads.

For the crochet trimming :—

First Row.—1 treble into a picot of braid, 1 chain. Repeat.

Second Row.—1 cross treble, 2 chain, pass over 2 stitches, and repeat.

Section of Trimming for Apron.

Third Row.—5 double trebles under each 2 chain of last row.

Fourth Row.—Like second row.

Fifth Row.—1 treble into a stitch of last row, 1 chain. Repeat.

Sixth Row.—Like second row.

Seventh Row.—1 double into a cross treble, 6 chain. Repeat.

Eighth Row.—1 treble into fourth of 6 chain, 3 chain, 1 double into the first, 1 treble into same stitch the last was worked into, 1 chain, 5 double trebles under next 6 chain, 1 chain. Repeat.

Ninth Row.—1 double into 1 chain, 7 chain. Repeat. The eighth and ninth rows are repeated twice more.

Fourteenth Row.—Like eighth row.

Fifteenth Row.—1 double into 1 chain, 3 chain, 1 double into picot of last row, 3 chain, 1 double into next chain, pass over 1 stitch, 1 treble into the next, * 3 chain, 1 double into the first, 1 treble into next stitch, repeat from * twice more, working 2 trebles into the third of 5 double trebles of last row, 1 chain. Repeat from the beginning of the row. The side is finished by working 3 chain, 1 double into the first, 1 double into corner stitch of 5 trebles of fourteenth row. These little picots are continued up the side (see design.)

Parasol Cover Crocheted.

Finlayson, Bousfield & Co.'s, REAL SCOTCH CROCHET THREAD, No. 60, quite a good size bone hook. Commence at part goes over top of parasol.

1st round.—Fasten the thread in the ninth stitch of the ch an l make 11 ch, 1 dc under the ch; * 11 ch, 1 dc under the same ch, repeat from * 11 times; break off.

2nd round.—Fasten in the sixth loop of the 11 ch and make 5 ch, * 1 dc in the next 11 ch, 5 ch; repeat from * all around; join with a dc in the same loop as in beginning the row,

3rd round.—Work along the 5 ch of preceding row in sc (single crochet) until the centre stitch of the loop is reached, then make * ch, 1 dc in the next 5 ch; repeat from * all round; join with a dc as in second round. These three rounds form an open star around the top of the parasol.

4th round.—This round is worked in 5 groups of long chains forming fans with an intervening ch between each group. There are 6 fans around: 11 ch, 1 dc in the third stitch of the 5 ch of preceding row; * 11 ch, 1 dc in the same stitch; 11 ch, 1 dc in the same stitch; repeat the 11 ch twice more, making a groop of 5 chains in all; 12 ch, miss 5 (one space), 1 dc in the third of the next 5 ch; 11 ch; repeat from * all round.

5th round.—Work in sc until you have reached the sixth stitch of the 11 ch; * make 5 ch, 1 dc in the next 11 ch; 5 ch, 1 dc in the next 11 ch; repeat the chains 3 times more; 5 ch, miss 5, 1 dc in the next stitch; repeat from * all around.

6th round.—5 ch, 1 dc in the third of the 5 ch of preceding row; 5 ch, 1 dc in the next 5 ch; repeat.

7th round.—* 12 ch, 1 dc in the third of the 5 ch; 12 ch, 1 dc in the same stitch; 5 ch, 1 dc in the next 5 ch; repeat from *.

8th round.—Work along the 12 ch in sc until you have reached the sixth loop; 1 dc in the middle of the next 12 ch; * 5 ch, 1 dc in the next 12 ch; 5 ch, 1 dc in the 12 ch; repeat from * around; join with a dc in the same stitch as in beginning the next round.

9th round.—* 5 ch, miss 5 ch, 1 dc in the dc on the next 12 ch ; repeat from * around.

10th round.—5 ch, 1 dc in the third of the first 5 ch ; 1 dc in the next 5 ch ; repeat all around.

11th round.—1 dc in every stitch.

12th round.—Work up 5 ch to take the place of a treble ; one treble in the next stitch ; * 2 ch, miss 1 stitch ; 1 treble in the next ; repeat from * ; join in the third stitch of the 5 ch.

13th round.—5 ch miss 1 treble, 1 dc in the next treble ; repeat round *.

14th round.—5 ch ; * miss 4 stitches, 1 dc in the next ; 5 ch ; repeat from *.

15th round—Like the seventh.

16th round.—Like the eighth.

17th round.—Like the ninth.

18th round.—5 ch, 1 dc in the third of the next 5 ch ; 4 ch, 1 dc in the same loop ; 5 ch, 1 dc in the next 5 ch ; repeat all round. Break off.

This completes the lace for the upper half of parasol.

THE BORDER.

The wide border which covers the lower half of the parasol consists of one row of large ornamental squares and one row of pineapples below the squares. The squares are worked in this way : Make a chain of 5 stitches and join into a ring.

1st round.—Work up 7 ch, to take the place of a treble, and under the ring work 4 groups of 5 trebles each, separated by 5 ch ; join in the fourth stitch of the seventh ch.

2nd round.—2 dcs in each stitch of the 5 ch, 2 dcs between each of the trebles ; repeat all round.

3rd round.—4 ch, to take the place of a treble ; 1 treble in the next stitch ; * 2 ch, miss 1, 1 treble in the next stitch ; repeat from * all round, except on each corner where you make 3 ch and treble in the next 2 dcs, instead of missing one stitch.

4th round.—5 ch, 1 dc in the same loop ; * 5 ch, miss 2 trebles, 1 dc in the next stitch ; repeat from * all around, except on the corners where you make 5 ch, 1 dc in the same loop. This completes one square. Make 15 more like it, arrange them around the parasol, sewing them on below the lace work already described and joining the opposite points that run diagonally across the squares. The last row of pineapples around the bottom of the parasol is made thus : Make a chain of five stitches.

First Row.—Miss 4 in the fifth loop work 3 trebles, 2 ch, 3 trebles ; this forms one shell ; turn.

Second Row.—3 ch, 3 trebles, 2 ch, 3 trebles all under the 2 ch of first shell ; treble on last treble of shell ; turn.

Repeat the second row until you have made a strip of 10 shells. Under this strip a scallop is worked, with the pineapples in the centre. This begins on the eleventh row.

Eleventh Row.—5 ch, miss 2 shells; 3 trebles, 2 ch, 3 trebles (forming one shell), all under the 3 ch between eighth and ninth shells; 4 ch, miss 3, 3 trebles, 2 ch, 3 trebles, all on the treble between fourth and sixth shells; 4 ch, miss 3 shells, 1 shell (3 tr, 2 ch, 3 tr as before) under 3 ch between second and third shells; 5 ch 1 sc (single crochet) under first treble of last shell; turn. There are now 3 shells along the edge of the strip of 10 shells. A row of shells is to be worked in the first and third of these shells, while the middle one forms the foundation for the pineapple.

Twelfth Row.—10 d cs under the 5 ch; 1 ch, 1 shell on first shell; 4 ch, 10 trebles under 2 ch of second shell; 4 ch, 1 shell on third shell; 5 ch, 1 sc on 1 ch after last shell; turn.

Thirteenth Row.—Work along this 5 ch in sc until the first shell is reached; then 1 ch, shell on shell; 4 ch, 1 dc between the first and second trebles; * 2 ch, 1 dc between the next 2 trebles; repeat from * until there are 9 d cs in all, the last being between the ninth and tenth trebles; then 4 ch, shell on shell, 5 ch, 1 sc under 1 ch after shell; turn.

Fourteenth Row.—10 d cs under 5 ch; 1 ch shell on shell; 3 ch, 1 dc under first 2 ch; * 2 ch, 1 dc under next 2 ch; repeat from * until there are 8 d cs, then 3 ch, shell on shell; 5 ch, 1 sc under 1 ch after shell; turn.

Fifteenth Row.—Work back along the 5 ch until first shell is reached, then 1 ch, shell on shell; 3 ch, 1 dc under first 2 ch; * 2 ch, 1 dc under next 2 ch, repeat from * until there are 7 d cs; 3 ch, shell on shell; 5 ch, 1 sc under 1 ch after shell; turn.

Sixteenth Row.—Like fourteenth, except that there are only 6 d cs in pineapple instead of 8 dcs.

Seventeenth Row.—Like fifteenth, but 5 d cs instead of 7 d cs.

Eighteenth Row.—Like sixteenth; but only 4 d cs.

Nineteenth Row.—Work back along the 5 ch to first shell; 1 ch, shell on shell, 3 ch, 1 dc under 2 ch; 2 ch, 1 dc under next 2 ch; 2 ch, 1 dc under next 2 ch; 3 ch, shell on shell; 5 ch, 1 sc under 1 ch; turn.

Twentieth Row.—10 d cs under 5 ch; 1 ch, shell on shell; 3 ch, 1 dc under first 2 ch; 2 ch 1 dc under next 2 ch; 3 ch, shell on shell; 5 ch, 1 sc under 1 ch; turn.

Twenty-first Row.—sc along the 5 ch to first shell; 1 ch, shell on shell; 3 ch, work along the 3 ch in sc, then shell on shell; 5 ch, 1 sc under 1 ch; turn. The pineapple is now completed and the two parts of the scallop are to be joined.

Twenty-second Row.—10 d cs under 5 ch; 5 ch, 1 sc under the 1 ch beyond the first shell worked in the last row, or between the first 2 shells of the other half of the scallop. This joins the two sets of shells. Now, instead of working back along the ch turn, work in sc on the first 3 trebles of the first shell and the last 3 trebles of the second shell, or 6 trebles in all, joining the third and fourth trebles together by putting the hook through both and working off the 3 loops as one sc. This brings you to the outer edge of the last made shell, where the last 5 ch started; turn.

Twenty-third row.—10 d cs under 5 ch; 1 sc under 1 ch; 10 d cs under each of the other 5 ch along this half of the scallop, with a sc under each 1 ch between them. This finishes the scallop. Now 1 ch, shell on the last shell of the upper strip. Turn and continue working as at first until there are again 10 shells, when you start the second scallop by repeating from the eleventh row. The first four loops on the edge of each scallop are to be joined in the working to last four loops of the previous scallop by working 5 d cs then taking the hook out, putting it through the middle dc of previous scallop, drawing the loop through and finishing the 10 d cs as usual.

The upper half of the cover is tacked along the upper part of parasol. The squares are sewn on below this last round, and then the pineapples, the points of the scallop coming to within half an inch of the edge of the parasol.

Rose Tidy or Cushion Cover.

Use fine number of Finlayson, Bousfield & Co.'s REAL SCOTCH CRO-CHET THREAD. Make circle of 20 chain stitches.

1st round.—30 double crochets worked over the ring.

2nd round.—Double crochet all around, widening in six places to make 36 d cs in all.

3rd round.—1 * dc 5 chain, miss 1, *, repeat all around from * to *.

4th round.—1 double crochet on the middle stitch of 5 chain of preceding row, 5 chain and 1 dc on middle of next chain of 5; repeat all round.

5th round.—Double crochet all around, 1 in each stitch and 3 in middle of each chain of 5.

6th round.—Double crochet all around, with 3 in each loop of 3 of preceding row. The seventh, eighth ninth, tenth and eleventh rounds are like the eighth, and form the raised petals of the flower.

12th round.—One double crochet, between two petals, or scallops, taking up the two middle stitches, make 5 chain put 1 dc between next 2 petals, continue this all around. There should be 18 five-chain loops in all.

13th round.—One double crochet in the middle of each loop with 5 chain between. Make fourteenth, fifteenth and sixteenth rounds in the same manner as thirteenth, increasing the number of chain stitches between d cs enough to keep the circle flat.

17th round.—One treble in the first loop, make chain of one less chain than in immediately preceding row, i. e., if chain then was increased to 6, put 7 in this row. * 1 treble in the next loop, in the top of this treble stitch make 3 double crochets, with 3 chain between each 7 chain, * repeat from * to * all round. The 3 ch, 1 dc worked 3 times on top of each treble stitch makes a pretty trefoil edge to the circle.

For a round tidy make seven of these circles, put one in the middle with six others around it. Fill the open spaces with little circles made by chaining a ring of 10 stitches.

1st round.—10 double crochets.

2nd round.—1 treble, 3 chain, miss 1; repeat 7 times.

3rd round.—9 treble over each loop of 3 chain, 1 double crochet worked between.

For larger circles to go on the spaces outside of the 6 flower circles add a fourth round to the three just given.

4th round.—One treble in the middle of each scallop; on the top of the treble work 3 dc with 3 chain between each dc (trefoil edge), then chain 6 and repeat all around.

To make a border for the tidy:

1st round.—Make 1 treble in 1 of the trefoils of flat circle, 8 chain, 1 treble in next trefoil, 8 chain, 1 long treble in the third trefoil, 10 chain, 1 long in first trefoil of large circle, 1 treble in each of the next, 4 trefoils of large circle with 8 chain between each, 8 chain, 1 long in the next trefoil of large circle, 10 chain, 1 long on the first trefoil of the next small circle, 8 chain, repeat from beginning.

2nd round.—2 treble with 1 chain between in first stitch of last round, * 4 chain, miss 5, 2 treble with 1 chain between in the next stitch, repeat from *.

3rd round.—Same as second, with the 2 treble stitches always under the 1 chain of previous round.

4th round.—Seam as third.

5th round.—4 treble under each 1 chain, with 1 chain between the second and third, 4 chains, repeat. This is like the first 4 rounds, except that the trebles are in groups of 4, instead of 2, under each 1 chain.

6th round.—Like fifth.

7th round.—1 treble in 1 chain, 1 trefoil, made as in seventeenth row of flower circles, on the top of treble, 6 chain; repeat all around.

Another Pin Cushion Cover Crocheted.

No. 70 Finlayson, Bousfield & Co.'s REAL SCOTCH CROCHET THREAD, fine steel hook.

To make a picot is to make a chain of five loops, put the hook through the first loop, catch the thread and draw through both loops on hook at once. A smaller picot may be made with 3 chain.

Make a chain of 9 stitches and join into a ring.

1st round.— * 12 chain, 1 double crochet into the ring ; repeat from * eleven times, making in all of 12 long loops 12 chain each, and break off or work to the middle of first long loop in single crochet.

2nd round.—* Start in the sixth loop of the first 12 chain with a double crochet, 5 chain, 1 double crochet in the sixth loop of the next 12 chain ; repeat from * closing with a double crochet with which the round began.

3rd round.—Single crochet until the middle of the first 5 chain is reached, then 1 double crochet under first 5 chain, * 7 chain, 1 double crochet under next 5 chain, * repeat from * to * all round.

4th round.—13 chain, 1 double crochet under first 7 chain, * 12 chain, 1 double crochet under same 7 chain *; repeat from * to * 4 times ; 13 chain, 1 double crochet into next 7 chain, * 12 chain, 1 double crochet under same 7 chain *; repeat from last * to * 4 times. Continue round in this way, making 6 groups in all, and break off or work in single crochet to middle of first long loop.

5th round.—Begin with a double crochet on top of first 13 chain, 5 chain, 1 double crochet on top of 12 chain, 5 chain on top of next 12 chain ; repeat all round, working a double crochet on top of each long chain.

6th round.—1 double crochet under first 5 chain, * 5 chain, 1 double crochet under next 5 chain ; * repeat from * to * all round.

7th round.—1 double crochet under first 5 chain, * 5 chain, picot of 3, 1 treble under next 5 chain, 1 picot on top of this treble, 1 picot after treble, 5 chain, 1 double crochet under next 5 chain ; * repeat from * to *.

For small rosettes to use in joining the large ones :

Make a chain of 9 stitches and join into a ring.

1st round.--16 double crochet under the ring.

2nd round.--1 treble on first double crochet, 5 chain, miss 1 double crochet, 1 treble on next double crochet ; repeat.

3rd round.—Under each 5 chain work 7 double crochet.

4th round.—1 treble in fourth of first 7 double crochet, 3 picots of 3 chain each on top of this first treble, 6 chain, * picot of 3, 1 treble on the fourth of next 7 double crochet, 2 picots of 3 chain each on top of treble, 6 chain * repeat from * to * all round.

Arrange the large rosettes in 3 rows of 3 each, and put two of the small ones between the first and second rows, the other two between the second and third rows. Each of the small rosettes is thus surrounded by four large ones. The rosettes are all joined at the tops of the little clusters of 2 picots.

Tack this cover on the top of a cushion of bright-colored satin, velvet, or plush. Add a bow of ribbon at each corner of the cushion.

Nine of these large rosettes will make a small tidy.

Tidy of Darned Net.

See page 39 for Cut.

Work on net with Finlayson, Bousfield & Co.'s linen floss, colored or white.
This design shows three different designs, which is made by counting the
holes. When all done, sew on a pearl edge all around tidy. This edge comes
on purpose.

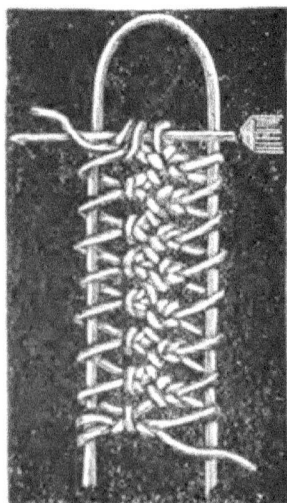

Hair-Pin Work.

Get a good-size common hair-pin, though bone ones are used. Use Finlayson, Bousfield & Co.'s REAL SCOTCH CROCHET THREAD, coarse or
fine, as desired.

To commence, hold the hair-pin in the left hand, the round part upwards,
twist the cotton round the left prong, pass it over the right prong to the back of
the hair-pin, and lay it over the left forefinger. Take up a crochet hook and
draw this back thread to the front under the first crossed one, and make a chain
by taking up fresh cotton and pulling it through. Take the hook out and turn
the hair-pin; * the cotton will now be in front; put it over the right hand pin to
the back, hook into loop, and make a chain by drawing the cotton through, then
put the hook through the twist on the left hand prong, and make a chain having

two stitches on the hook, make a stitch drawing cotton through these two loops, so that only one loop is left. Take out the hook, turn the work, and repeat from *. When the hair-pin is filled with work slip it off; to steady the prong ends put them through some of the last loops, and continue to work as before. Work that is well done of this kind has large open loops at the sides of uniform length.

Hair Pin Lace, Crocheted.

With Finlayson, Bonsfield & Co.'s REAL SCOTCH CROCHET THREAD No. 16 make two pieces of hair-pin work, length desired. Join with CROCHET LINEN THREAD, as seen, and on bottom of same coarse thread work the scallop. This is very pretty for the bottom of aprons. When used to trim an apron run the scallop up each side of the edging, but not the apron. This idea was taken from *Harper's Bazaar.*

A Knitted Tidy.

[Madam Goubaud.]

Use No. 16 or finer Finlayson, Bousfield & Co.'s, REAL SCOTCH CRO-
CHET THREAD. Four No. 16 steel needles. Cast on 4 stitches, join them
into a circle, and work the first round, four times alternately, make 1, knit 1
plain.

2nd round.—Plain knitting.

3rd round.—* make 1, 1 plain *, repeat from * to * 7 times, after every pattern round knit 1 round plain. This will not be mentioned again until after
twenty-first round.

5th round.—* make 1, 2 plain. * Repeat from * to *.

From the seventh to the twelfth round the knitted stitches in every other
round increase by 1 stitch, so that in the twelfth round there are 7 stitches between those formed by make 1.

13th round.—* make 1, narrow, 4 plain, narrow.* Repeat from * to *.

15th round.—* make 1, 1 plain, make 1, narrow, 2 plain, narrow.* Repeat
from * to *.

17th round.—* make 1, 3 plain, make 1, narrow, narrow.* Repeat from * to *.

19th round.—* make 1, 5 plain, make 1, narrow.* Repeat from * to *.

21st round.—* 1 plain, make 1, 5 plain, make 1, 2 plain.* Repeat from * to *.

22nd round.—* 1 plain, narrow, 1 plain, narrow, 3 plain.* Repeat from * to *.

23d round.—* 1 plain, make 1, 3 plain, make 1, 3 plain.* Repeat from * to *.

24th round.—* 3 plain, narrow, 5 plain.* Repeat from * to *.

25th round.—* 3 plain, make 1, narrow, make 1, 4 plain.* Repeat from * to *.

26th round.—All plain.

27th round.—* make 1, 9 plain, make 1, 1 plain.* Repeat from * to *.

28th round.—All plain.

29th round.—* 1 plain, make 1, 9 plain, make 1, 2 plain.* Repeat from * to *.

30th round.—All plain.

31st round.—* 2 plain, make 1, 9 plain, make 1, 3 plain.* Repeat from * to *.

32nd round.—All plain.

33rd round.—* 3 plain, make 1, 9 plain, make 1, 4 plain.* Repeat all round.

34th round.—* 4 plain, narrow, 5 plain, narrow, 5 plain.* Repeat all round.

35th round.—* 4 plain, make 1, 7 plain, make 1, 5 plain.* Repeat all round.

36th round.—* 5 plain, narrow, 3 plain, narrow, 6 plain.* Repeat all round.

37th round.—* make 1, 5 plain, make 1, 5 plain, make 1, 5 plain, make 1, 1
plain.* Repeat all round.

38th round.—* 7 plain, narrow, 1 plain, narrow, 8 plain.* Repeat all round.

39th round.—* 1 plain, make 1, 6 plain, make 1, 3 plain, make 1, 6 plain,
make 1, 2 plain.* Repeat all round.

40th round.—* 9 plain, knit 3 together, 10 plain.* Repeat all round.

41st round.—* 2 plain, make 1, 15 plain, make 1, 3 plain.* Repeat all round.

42nd round.—* 3 plain, narrow, 11 plain, narrow, 4 plain.* Repeat all
round.

43rd round. — * 3 plain, make 1, 13 plain, make 1, 4 plain.* Repeat all round.

44th round.—* 4 plain, narrow, 9 plain, narrow, 5 plain.* Repeat all round.
Bind off loosely. Make the following edge separately and sew on to tidy.
Cast on 5 stitches, knit across plain once,

First Row.—Slip 1, make 1, narrow, make 1, 2 plain.

Second Row.—Slip 1, rest plain. Every even row like second row.

Third Row.—Slip 1, make 1, narrow, make 1, narrow, make 1, 1 plain.

Fifth Row.—Slip 1, make 1, narrow, make 1, narrow, make 1, 2 plain.

Seventh Row.—Slip 1 (make 1, narrow) 3 times, make 1, 1 plain.

Ninth Row. — Slip 1, (make 1, narrow) 3 times, make 1, 2 plain.

Eleventh Row.—Slip 1, (make 1, narrow) 4 times, knit 1 plain.

Thirteenth Row. — Slip 1, (make 1, narrow) 4 times, make 1, 2 plain.

Fifteenth Row. — Bind off 8 stitches, make 1, narrow, make 1, 1 plain.

Sixteenth Row. — All plain.

Begin at 1st row and knit a piece long enough for tidy, to trim all round.

Knitted Diamond.

[For Tidy].

Use Finlayson, Bousfield & Co.'s, No. 16, REAL SCOTCH CROCHET THREAD, two No. 16 steel needles. When sewed together line tidy with some bright color and tie in fringe or trim with balls.

Cast on one stitch.

Second row.—Make 1, knit 1 plain. (After this the word stitches is understood.)

Third row.—Make 1, seam 2.
Fourth row.—Make 1, 3 plain.
Fifth row.—Make 1, seam 4.
Sixth row.—Make 1, 5 plain.
Seventh row.—Make 1, seam 6.
Eighth row.—Make 1, 7 plain.
Ninth row.—Make 1, seam 8.
Tenth row.—Make 1, 9 plain.
Eleventh row.—Make 1, seam 10.
Twelfth row.—Make 1, seam 11.
Thirteenth row.—Make 1, 12 plain.
Fourteenth row.—Make 1, 13 plain.
Fifteenth row.—Make 1, seam 14.
Sixteenth row.—Make 1, seam 15.
Seventeenth row.—Make 1, 16 plain. You now have 17 stitches on needle.

Eighteenth row.—* make 1, narrow.* Repeat from * to * all across until last stitch, then make 1, 1 plain.

Nineteenth row.—Make 1, seam 18.
Twentieth row.—Make 1, seam 19.
Twenty-first row.—Make 1, 20 plain.
Twenty-second row.—* make 1, narrow.* Repeat from * to * all across till last stitch, then make 1, 1 plain.

Twenty-third row.—Make 1, seam 22.
Twenty-fourth row.—Make 1, seam 23.
Twenty-fifth row.—Make 1, 24 plain.
Twenty-sixth row.—Make 1, 25 plain.
Twenty-seventh row.—Make 1, seam 26.
Twenty-eighth row.—Make 1, * 2 plain, seam 2.* Repeat from * to * across till last stitch, which is seamed.

Twenty-ninth row.—Make 1, 1 plain, * seam 2, 2 plain.* Repeat from * to * all across till last stitch, which is plain.

Thirtieth row.—Make 1, 1 plain, * seam 2, 2 plain, *. Repeat from * to * across.

Thirty-first row.—Make 1, * seam 2, 2 plain, *. Repeat from * to * across.

Thirty-second row.—Make 1, * seam 2, 2 plain, *. Repeat from * to * to last stitch, which is plain.

Thirty-third row.—Make 1, seam 1, * 2 plain, seam 2.* Repeat from * to * to last stitch, which is seamed.

Thirty-fourth row.—Make 1, seam 1, * 2 plain, seam 2 *. Repeat from * to *.

Thirty-fifth row.—Make 1, * 2 plain, seam 2.* Repeat from * to * across.

Thirty-sixth row.—Make 1, 35 plain.
Thirty-seventh row.—Make 1, seam 36.
Thirty-eighth row.—Make 1, seam 37.
Thirty-ninth row.—Make 1, 38 plain.

Fortieth row.—* Make 1, narrow.* Repeat from * to * all across till last stitch, then make 1, 1 plain (40 stitches here).

Forty-first row.—Make 1, seam 40.
Forty-second row.—Make 1, seam 41.
Forty-third row.—Make 1, 42 plain.
Forty-fourth row.—* Make 1, narrow.* Repeat from * to * till last stitch, which knit plain.

Forty-fifth row.—Make 1, seam 44.

Forty-sixth row.—Make 1, seam 45.

Forty-seventh row.—Make 1, 46 plain.

Forty-eighth row.—Make 1, 47 plain.

Forty-ninth row.—Make 1, seam 48.

Fiftieth row.—Make 1, * 6 plain, seam 6.* Repeat from * to * till last stitch, which is plain.

Fifty-first row.—Make 1, * 6 plain, seam 6.* Repeat from * to * to last 2 stitches, which are plain.

Fifty-second row.—Make 1, seam 3, * 6 plain, seam 6.* Repeat from * to * across.

Fifty-third row.—Make 1, 5 plain, * seam 6, 6 plain,* Repeat from * to * till last 5, which are plain.

Fifty-fourth row.—Make 1, * seam 6, 6 plain.* Repeat from * to * till last 5, which are seamed.

Fifty-fifth row.—Plain knitting.

Fifty-sixth row.— Slip 1, 1 plain, pass slipped stitch over, 5 plain, * seam 6, 6 plain.* Repeat from * to * till last 5, which are plain.

Fifty-seventh row.—Slip and bind as before, seam 4, * 6 plain, seam 6.* Repeat from * to * till last 5, which are seamed.

Fifty-eighth row.—Slip and bind, 2 plain, * seam 6, 6 plain.* Repeat from * to *.

Fifty-ninth row.— Slip and bind, seam 5, * 6 plain, seam 6.* Repeat from * to * to last 2, which are seamed.

Sixtieth row. — Slip and bind, knit 48 stitches plain (49 now on needle).

Sixty-first row.—Slip and bind, seam 47.

Sixty-second row. — Slip and bind, seam 46.

Sixty-third row.—Slip and bind, 45 plain.

Sixty-fourth row. — Slip and bind, * narrow, make 1, * repeat from * to *.

Sixty-fifth row.—Slip and bind, seam 43.

Sixty-sixth row. — Slip and bind, seam 42

Sixty-seventh row.—Slip and bind, 41 plain.

Sixty-eighth row.—Slip and bind, * narrow, make 1 *, repeat from * to *.

Sixty-ninth row. — Slip and bind seam 39.

Seventieth row.—Slip and bind, seam 38.

Seventy-first row.—Slip and bind, 37 plain.

Seventy-second row.—Slip and bind, 36 plain.

Seventy-third row.—Slip and bind, seam 35.

Seventy-fourth row.—Slip and bind. *2 plain, seam 2.* Repeat from * to * across.

Seventy-fifth row.—Slip and bind, *2 plain, seam 2.* Repeat from * to * till last 1, which is plain.

Seventy-sixth row.—Slip and bind, * seam 1, 2 plain.* Repeat from * to * till last 1, which is seamed.

Seventy-seventh row.—Slip and bind, seam 1, * 2 plain, seam 2.* Repeat from * to *.

Seventy-eighth row.—Slip and bind, *seam 2, 2 plain.* Repeat from * to *.

Seventy-ninth row.—Slip and bind, * seam 2, 2 plain.* Repeat from * to * till last 1, which seam.

Eightieth row. — Slip and bind, 1 plain, * seam 2, 2 plain.* Repeat from * to * till last 1, which is plain.

Eighty-first row.—Slip and bind, 1

plain, * seam 2, 2 plain.* Repeat from * to *.

Eighty-second row.—Slip and bind, 26 plain.

Eighty-third row.—Slip and bind, seam 25.

Eighty-fourth row.—Slip and bind, seam 24.

Eighty-fifth row.—Slip and bind, 23 plain.

Eighty-sixth row.—Slip and bind, * make 1, narrow.* Repeat from * to *.

Eighty-seventh row.—Slip and bind, seam 21.

Eighty-eighth row.—Slip and bind, seam 20.

Eighty-ninth row.—Slip and bind, 19 plain.

Ninetieth row.—Slip and bind, * narrow, make 1.* Repeat from * to *.

Ninety-first row.—Slip and bind, seam 17.

Ninety-second row.—Slip and bind, seam 16.

Ninety-third row.—Slip and bind, 15 plain.

Ninety-fourth row.—Slip and bind, 14 plain.

Ninety-fifth row.—Slip and bind, seam 13.

Ninety-sixth row.—Slip and bind, seam 12.

Ninety-seventh row.—Slip and bind, 11 plain.

Ninety-eighth row.—Slip and bind, 10 plain.

Ninety-ninth row.—Slip and bind, seam 9.

One Hundredth row.—Slip and bind, 8 plain.

One Hundred and First row.—Slip and bind, seam 7.

One Hundred and Second row.—Slip and bind, 6 plain.

One Hundred and Third row.—Slip and bind, 5 plain.

One Hundred and Fourth row.—Slip and bind, 4 plain.

One Hundred and Fifth row.—Slip and bind, seam 3.

One Hundred and Sixth row.—Slip and bind, 2 plain.

One Hundred and Seventh row.—Slip and bind, 1 plain.

One Hundred and Eighth row.—Bind off.

Knitted Square for Tidy.

Same materials or finer if wished as was used in the diamond.   From Madame Goubaud.

Cast on 8 stitches, 2 on each of 4 needles, join, and knit 1 round plain.

2nd round.—* 1 plain, make 1, 1 plain, * repeat from * to * all round.

Every odd round all plain.

4th round.— * 1 plain, make 1, 1 plain, make 1, 1 plain, * repeat from * to * all round.

6th round.—* 1 plain, make 1, 3 plain, make 1, 1 plain, * repeat from * to * all round.

8th round.—" 1 plain, make 1, 5 plain, make 1, 1 plain, * repeat from * to * all round.

10th round.—"1 plain, make 1, 7 plain, make 1, 1 plain, * repeat from * to * all round.

12th round.—" 1 plain, make 1, 9 plain, make 1, 1 plain, * repeat from * to * all round.

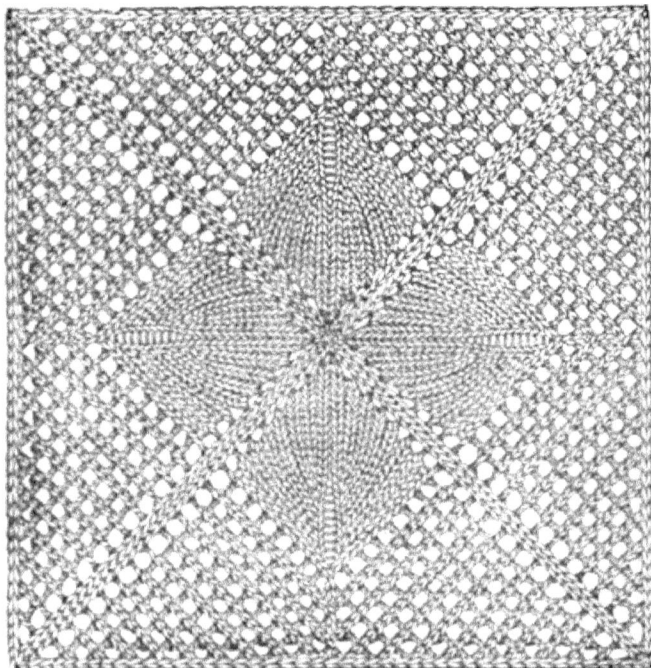

14th round.—" 1 plain, make 1, 11 plain, make 1, 1 plain, * repeat from * to * all round.

16th round.—" 1 plain, make 1, 13 plain, make 1, 1 plain, * repeat from * to * all round.

18th round.—" 1 plain, make 1, 15 plain, make 1, 1 plain, * repeat from * to * all round.

20th round.—" 1 plain, make 1, 1 plain, make 1, 5 plain, slip 1, 1 plain, pass slipped stitch over, 1 plain, narrow, 5 plain, make 1, 1 plain, make 1, 1 plain, * repeat from * to * all round.

22nd round.--* 1 plain, make 1, 1 plain, make 1, slip 1, 1 plain, pass slipped stitch over, make 1, 4 plain, slip 1, 1 plain, pass slipped stitch over, 1 plain, narrow, 4 plain, make 1, narrow, make 1, 1 plain, make 1, 1 plain, * repeat from * to * all round.

24th round.—* 1 plain, make 1, 1 plain, make 1, * slip 1, 1 plain, pass slipped stitch over, make 1, repeat from last * 3 plain, slip 1, 1 plain, pass slipped stich over, 1 plain, narrow, 3 plain, * make 1, narrow, * repeat from last * to * till last 2 stitches, make 1, 1 plain, make 1, 1 plain, * repeat from first * to last * all round.

26th round.—* 1 plain, make 1, 1 plain, make 1, * slip 1, 1 plain, pass slipped stitch over, make 1, repeat from last * twice 2 plain, slip 1, 1 plain, pass slipped stitch over, 1 plain, narrow, 2 plain, * make 1, narrow, repeat from last * twice, make 1, 1 plain, make 1, 1 plain, * repeat from first * to last * all round.

28th round.—*1 plain, make 1, 1 plain, make 1, * slip 1, 1 plain, pass slipped stitch over, make 1, repeat from last * 3 times, 1 plain, slip 1, pass slipped stitch over, 1 plain, narrow, 1 plain (make 1, narrow) 4 times, make 1, 1 plain, make 1, 1 plain, * repeat from first * to last * all round.

30th round.—1 plain, make 1, 1 plain, make 1, (slip 1, 1 plain, pass slipped stitch over) six times, (1 plain, narrow, make 1) six times, 1 plain, make 1, 1 plain, * repeat from * to * all round.

32nd round.—* 1 plain, make 1 repeat, (slip 1, 1 plain, pass slipped stitch over, make 1) 6 times, knit 3 together, then (make 1, narrow) 6 times, make 1, 1 plain, make 1, 1 plain, * repeat from * to * all round.

34th round.—* 1 plain, make 1, 1 plain, then (make 1, slip 1, 1 plain, pass slipped stitch over) 7 times, 1 plain, (narrow, make 1) 7 times, 1 plain, make 1, 1 plain, * repeat from * to * all round.

36th round.—* 1 plain, make 1, (1 plain, make 1, slip 1, 1 plain, pass slipped stitch over, make 1) seven times, knit 3 together, (make 1, narrow) 7 times, make 1, 1 plain, make 1, 1 plain, * repeat from * to * all round.

38th round.—* 1 plain, make 1, 1 plain, (make 1, slip 1, 1 plain, pass slipped stitch over) 8 times, 1 plain, (narrow, make 1) 8 times, 1 plain, make 1, 1 plain, * repeat from * to *.

40th round.—* 1 plain, make 1, 1 plain, make 1, (slip 1, one plain, pass slipped stitch over, make 1) 8 times, knit 3 together, (make 1, narrow) 8 times, make 1, 1 plain, make 1, 1 plain, * repeat from * to * all round.

50th round.—All plain knitting. Bind off all round very loosely.

If one wishes, each of the 4 sections may be done separately on 2 needles then sewed together.

Normandy Lace.

Cast on thirty stitches. Knit across plain once.

First Row.—Knit 3, over, narrow, knit 4, narrow, over, knit 3, over, narrow, knit 7, narrow, over, knit 3, over, knit 2.

Second Row.—And every alternate row plain.

Third Row.—Knit 3, over, narrow, knit 3, narrow, over, knit 5, over, narrow, knit 5, narrow, over, knit 5, over, knit 2.

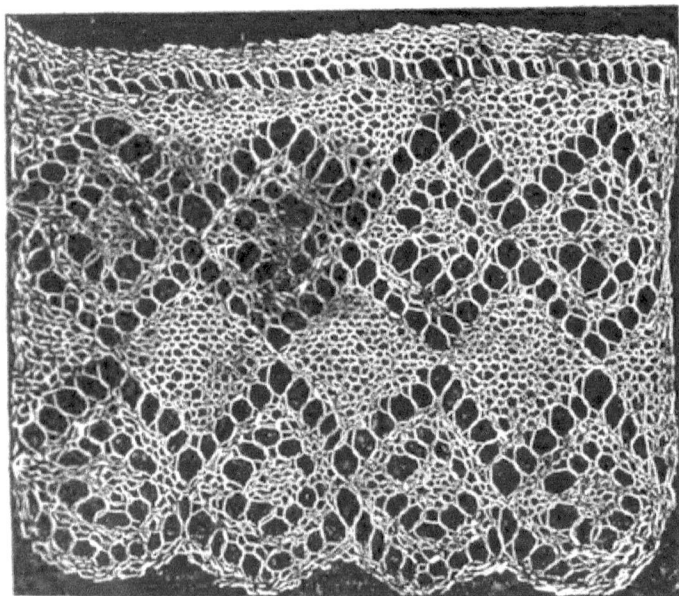

Fifth Row.—Knit 3, over, narrow, knit 2, narrow, over, narrow, knit 1, over, knit 1, over, narrow, knit 1, over, narrow, knit 3, narrow, over, narrow, knit 1, over, knit 1, over, narrow, knit 1, over, knit 2.

Seventh Row.—Knit 3, over, narrow, knit 1, narrow, over, narrow, knit 1, over, knit 3, over, narrow, knit 1, over, narrow, knit 1, narrow, over, narrow, knit 1, over, knit 3, over, narrow, knit 1, over, knit 2.

Ninth Row.—Knit 3, over, narrow, narrow, over, narrow, knit 1, over, knit 5, over, narrow, knit 1, over, slip, narrow, and bind (or narrow 3 stitches into 1), over, narrow, knit 1, over, knit 5, over, narrow, knit 1, over, knit 2.

Eleventh Row.—Knit 3, over, narrow, knit 2, over, narrow, knit 1, over, narrow, knit 1, narrow, over, narrow, knit 1, over, knit 3, over, narrow, knit 1, over, narrow, knit 1, narrow, over, narrow, knit 1, over, narrow, knit 1.

Thirteenth Row.—Knit 3, over, narrow, knit 3, over, narrow, knit 1, over, slip, narrow, and bind, over, narrow, knit 1, over, knit 5, over, narrow, knit 1, over, slip, narrow and bind, over, narrow, knit 1, over, narrow, knit 1.

Fifteenth Row.—Knit 3, over, narrow, knit 4, over, narrow, knit 3, narrow, over, knit 7, over, narrow, knit 3, narrow, over, narrow, knit 1.

Seventeenth Row.—Knit 3, over, narrow, knit 5, over, narrow, knit 1, narrow, over, knit 9, over, narrow, knit 1, narrow, over, narrow, knit 1.

Nineteenth Row.—Knit 3, over, narrow, knit 6, over, slip, narrow and bind, over, knit 11, over, slip, narrow and bind, over, narrow, knit 1.

INSERTION TO MATCH.

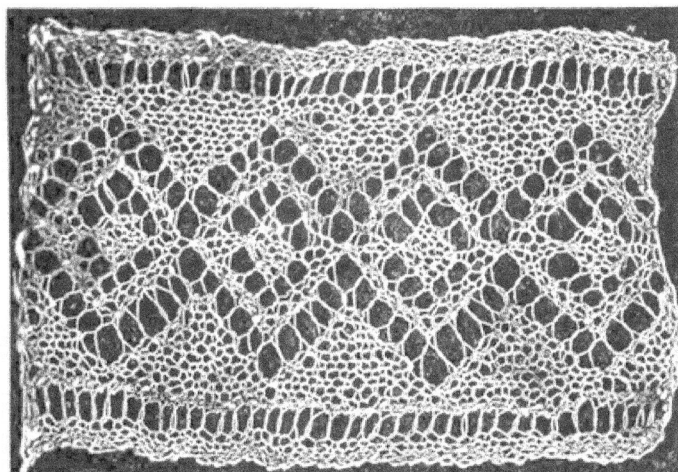

Cast on 25 stitches.

First Row.—Knit 3, over, narrow, knit 4, narrow, over, knit 3, over, narrow, knit 5, over, narrow, knit 2.

Second Row and every alternate row plain.

Third Row.—Knit 3, over, narrow, knit 3, narrow, over, knit 5, over, narrow, knit 4, over, narrow, knit 2.

Fifth Row.—Knit 3, over, narrow, knit 2, narrow, over, narrow, knit 1, over, knit 1, over, narrow, knit 1, over, narrow, knit 3, over, narrow, knit 2.

Seventh Row.—Knit 3, over, narrow, knit 1, narrow, over, narrow, knit 1, over knit 3, over, narrow, knit 1, over, narrow, knit 2, over, narrow, knit 2.

Ninth Row.—Knit 3, over, narrow, narrow, over, narrow, knit 1, over, knit 5, over narrow, knit 1, over, narrow, knit 1, over, narrow, knit 2.

Eleventh Row.—Knit 3, over, narrow, knit 2, over, narrow, knit 1, over, narrow, knit 1, narrow, over, narrow, knit 1, over, knit 3, over, narrow, knit 2.

Thirteenth Row.—Knit 3, over, narrow, knit 3, over, narrow, knit 1, over, slip, narrow and bind, over, narrow, knit 1, over, knit 4, over, narrow, knit 2.

Fifteenth Row.—Knit 3, over, narrow, knit 4, over narrow, knit 3, narrow, over, knit 5, over, narrow, knit 2.

Seventeenth Row.—Knit 3, over, narrow, knit 5, over, narrow, knit 1, narrow, over, knit 6, over, narrow, knit 2.

Nineteenth Row.—Knit 3, over, narrow, knit 6, over, slip, narrow and bind, over, knit 7, over, narrow, knit 2.

Use No. 50 Finlayson, Bousfield & Co.'s, REAL SCOTCH CROCHET THREAD. Two No. 16 needles.

Leaf Edging.

EXPLANATION OF TERMS.

t over 1, means thread over needle once, thus making 1 extra stitch.

t over 2, means thread over needle twice, thus making 2 extra stitches.

t over 3, means thread over needle 3 times, thus making 3 extra stitches.

Narrow, means knit 2 together.

First Row.—Cast on 30 stitches, knit across plain.

Second Row.—2 plain, t over 2, seam 2 stitches together; 6 plain, put 4 stitches over 1 stitch, t over 2, 2 plain, t over 2, seam 2 together, 1 plain, t over 2, narrow, knit plain to last 2 stitches, now t over 2, seam 2 stitches together.

Third Row.—Wind thread around needle once, seam 2 together, 8 plain, make 2 stitches of the double loop (by knitting one half plain and seaming other half) 1 plain, t over 2, seam 2 together, 2 plain, make 4 stitches of the double loop, by (taking one stitch and making ½ plain, ½ seam out of one stitch), 6 plain, t over 2, seam 2 together, 2 plain.

Fourth Row.—2 plain, t over 2, seam 2 together, 12 plain, t over 2, seam 2 together, knit plain till last 2, then t over 2, seam 2 together.

Fifth Row.—Wind thread around needle once, and seam 2 together, knit 11 plain, t over 2, seam 2 together, 6 plain, put 4 stitches over 1 stitch, t over 2, 2 plain, t over 2, seam 2 together, 2 plain.

Sixth Row.—2 plain, t over 2, seam 2 together, 2 plain, make 4 stitches of double loop, 6 plain, t over 2, seam 2 together, 1 plain, t over 2, narrow, knit plain until last 2 stitches, t over 2, seam 2 together.

Seventh Row.—Wind thread around needle once, seam 2 together, 7 plain, make 2 stitches of each double loop, 1 plain, t over 2, seam 2 together, 12 plain, t over 2, seam 2 together, 2 plain.

Eighth Row.—2 plain, t over 2, seam 2 together, 6 plain, put 4 stitches over 1 stitch, t over 2, 2 plain, t over 2, seam together, knit plain to last 2, t over 2, seam 2 together.

Ninth Row.—Wind thread around needle once, seam 2 together, 13 plain, t over 2, seam 2 together, 2 plain, make 4 stitches of double loop, 6 plain, t over 2, seam 2 together, 2 plain.

Tenth Row.—2 plain, t over 2, seam 2 together, 12 plain, t over 2, seam 2 together, 1 plain, t over 2, narrow, t over 2, narrow, t over 2, narrow, 1 plain, take one stitch from right-hand needle on to the left and slip every stitch on left needle over it till last 1; you now have 1 on left needle, which is knit plain.

Eleventh Row.—Wind thread around needle once, seam 2 together, 1 plain, make 2 stitches of every loop, 1 plain, t over 2, seam 2 together, 6 plain, put 4 over 1, 2 plain, t over 2, seam 2 together, 2 plain.

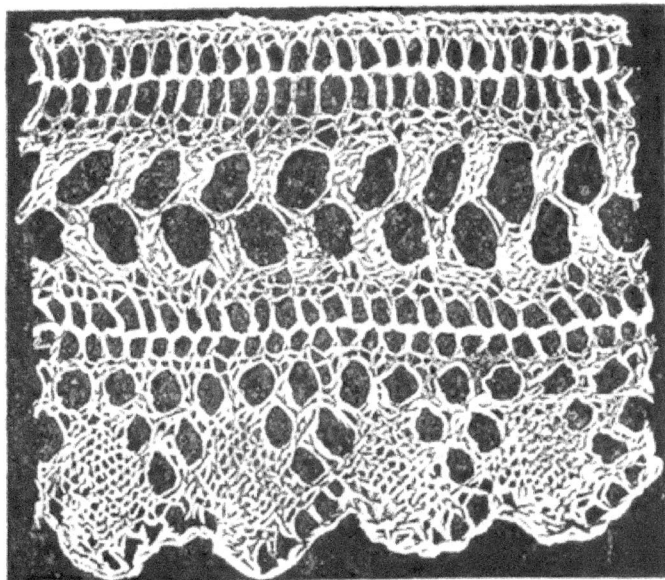

Twelfth Row.—2 plain, t over 2, seam 2 together, 2 plain, make 4 stitches of double loop, 6 plain, t over 2, seam 2 together, 2 plain, knit plain till last 2, t over 2, seam 2 together.

Thirteenth Row.—Wind thread around needle once, seam 2 together, 10 plain, t over 2, seam 2 together, 12 plain, t over 2, seam 2 together, 2 plain.

Some materials as Normandy lace only use No. 17 needles.

Wide Knitted Edge.

MATERIALS —Finlayson, Bousfield & Co.'s REAL SCOTCH CROCHET

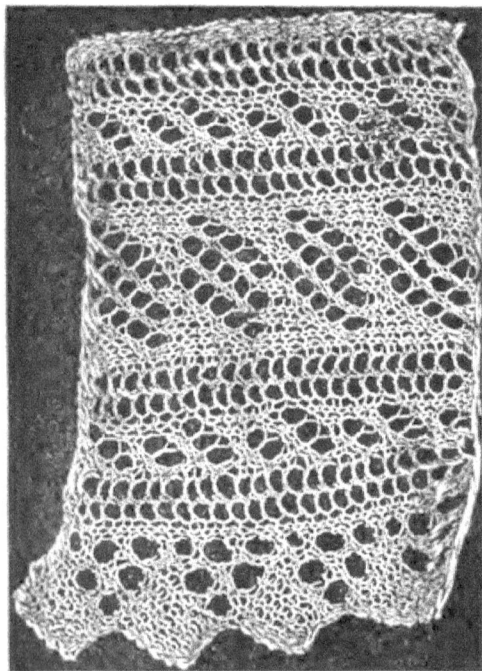

THREAD No. 70. Two No. 18 steel needles. Cast on 44 stitches, knit across plain once.

First Row.—3 plain, make 2, seam 2 together, 1 plain, make 1, narrow, 2 plain, make 2, seam 2 together, 2 plain, (make 1, narrow) 3 times, 5 plain, make 2, seam 2 together, 1 plain, make 1, narrow, 2 plain, make 2, seam 2 together, 2 plain, make 1, narrow, 6 plain.

Second Row.—7 plain, seam 1, 2 plain, make 2, seam 2 together, 5 plain, make 2, seam 2 together, 13 plain, make 2, seam 2 together, 5 plain, make 2, seam 2 together, 3 plain.

Third Row.—3 plain, make 2, seam 2 together, 2 plain, make 1, narrow, 1 plain, then make 2, seam 2 together, 3 plain, then (make 1, narrow) 3 times, 4 plain, make 2, seam 2 together, 2 plain, make 1, narrow, 1 plain, make 2, seam 2 together, 10 plain.

Fourth Row.—10 plain, make 2, seam 2 together, 5 plain, make 2, seam 2 together, 13 plain, make 2, seam 2 together, 5 plain, make 2, seam 2 together, 3 plain.

Fifth Row.—3 plain, make 2, seam 2 together, 3 plain, make 1, narrow, make 2, seam 2 together, 4 plain, (make 1, narrow) 3 times, 3 plain, make 2, seam 2 together, 3 plain, make 1, narrow, make 2, seam 2 together, 2 plain, make 2, narrow, make 2, 6 plain.

Sixth Row.—7 plain, seam 1, 2 plain, seam 1, 2 plain, make 2, seam 2 together, 5 plain, make 2, seam 2 together, 13 plain, make 2, seam 2 together, 5 plain, make 2, seam 2 together, 3 plain.

Seventh Row.—3 plain, make 2, seam 2 together, 5 plain, make 2, seam 2 together, 5 plain, (make 1, narrow) 3 times, 2 plain, make 2, seam 2 together, 5 plain, make 2, seam 2 together, 13 plain.

Eighth Row.—13 plain, make 2, seam 2 together, 5 plain, make 2, seam 2 together, 13 plain, make 2, seam 2 together, 5 plain, make 2, seam 2 together, 3 plain.

Ninth Row.—3 plain, make 2, seam 2 together, 2 plain, make 1, narrow, 1 plain, make 2, seam 2 together, 6 plain, (make 1, narrow) 3 times, 1 plain, make 2, seam 2 together, 2 plain, make 1, narrow, 1 plain, make 2, seam 2 together, 2 plain, (make 2, narrow) 3 times, then 5 plain.

Tenth Row.—16 plain, make 2, seam 2 together, 5 plain, make 2, seam 2 together, 13 plain, make 2, seam 2 together, 5 plain, make 2, seam 2 together, 3 plain.

Eleventh Row.—3 plain, make 2, seam 2 together, 3 plain, make 1, narrow, make 2, seam 2 together, 13 plain, make 2, seam 2 together, 3 plain, make 1, narrow, make 2, seam 2 together, 16 plain.

Twelfth Row.—Bind off 6, knit 9 plain, (besides 1 on needle, which makes 10) make 2, seam 2 together, 5 plain, make 2, seam 2 together, 13 plain, make 2, seam 2 together, 5 plain, make 2, seam 2 together, 3 plain. Repeat from first row.

Knitted Necktie.

Finlayson, Bousfield & Co.'s REAL SCOTCH CROCHET THREAD No. 60 or 70. Two steel needles No. 17. Cast on 25 stitches, knit across plain once.

First Row.—Knit plain.

Second Row.—Slip 1, narrow, knit 1, thread over, narrow, knit 1, thread over, narrow, knit 13, thread over, narrow, knit 1, thread over knit 3.

Third Row.—Slip 1, knit 9, over, narrow, knit 1 over, narrow, knit 13.

Fourth Row.—Like second row.

Fifth Row.—Slip 1, knit 11, over, narrow, knit 1, over, narrow, knit 11.

Sixth Row.—Like second.

Seventh Row.— Slip 1, knit 13, over, narrow, knit 1, over, narrow knit 9.

Eighth Row.—Like second.

Ninth Row.,—Slip 1, knit 15, over, narrow, knit 1 over, narrow knit 7.

This makes the pattern. Repeat from first row as long as will be required. For the end of the tie cast on 22 stitches.

First Row.—Knit 18, thread over twice, purl 2 together, knit 2.

Second Row.—Slip 1, knit 1, over twice, purl 2 together, knit 12, over, narrow, knit 1, over, knit 3.

Third Row.—Slip 1, knit 9, over, narrow, knit 1, over, narrow, knit 4, over twice, purl 2 together, knit 2.

Fourth Row.—Slip 1, knit 1, over twice, purl 2 together, knit 3, over, narrow, knit 1, over, knit 3.

Fifth Row.—Slip 1, knit 11, over, narrow, knit 1, over, narrow, knit 13, over twice, purl 2 together, knit 2.

Sixth Row.—Slip 1, knit 1, over twice, purl 2 together, knit 14, over, narrow, knit 1, over, knit 3.

Seventh Row.—Slip 1, knit 13, over, narrow, knit 1, over, narrow, knit 2, over twice, purl 2 together, knit 2.

Eighth Row.—Slip 1, knit 1, over twice, purl 2 together, knit 15, over, narrow, knit 1, over, knit 3.

Ninth Row.—Slip 1, knit 15, over, narrow, knit 1, over, narrow, knit 1, over twice, purl 2 together, knit 2.

Tenth Row.—Slip 1, knit 1, over twice, purl 2 together, knit all the rest plain.

Eleventh Row.—Slip 1, narrow, knit 1, over, narrow, knit 1, over, narrow, knit 13, over twice, purl 2 together, knit 2.

Twelfth Row.—Slip 1, knit 1, over twice, purl 2 together, knit 3, over, narrow, knit 1, over, narrow, knit 13.

Thirteenth Row.—Slip 1, narrow, knit 1, over, narrow 1, over, narrow, knit 12, over twice, purl 2 together, knit 2.

Fourteenth Row.—Slip 1, knit 1, over twice, purl 2 together, knit 4, over, narrow, knit 1, over, narrow, knit 11.

Fifteenth Row.—Slip 1, narrow, knit 1, over, narrow, knit 1, over, narrow, knit 11, over twice, purl 2 together, knit 2.

Sixteenth Row.—Slip 1, knit 1, over twice, purl 2 together, knit 5, over, narrow, knit 1, over, narrow, knit 9.

Seventeenth Row.—Slip 1, narrow, knit 1, over, narrow, knit 1, over, narrow, knit 10, over twice, purl 2 together, knit 2.

Eighteenth Row.—Slip 1, knit 1, over twice, purl 2 together, knit 6, over, narrow, knit 1, over, narrow, knit 7.

Knit 4 times through pattern, bind off loosely. Knit another piece the same and join neatly in middle of tie.

Swiss Lace Necktie, Knitted.

MATERIALS — Finlayson, Bousfield & Co.'s REAL SCOTCH CROCHET THREAD No. 50, two steel needles No. 16.

This is knit in two pieces and joined neatly in middle of tie. These ties are very pretty for morning wear, and caps of the same may be knitted in sections and sewed together.

Cast on 39 stitches, knit across plain.

First Row—Slip 1, 1 plain, t over 1, 5 plain, t over 1, narrow, 9 plain, narrow, t over 1, 5 plain, t over 1, narrow, 9 plain, narrow, t over 1, 5 plain, t over 1, 2 plain.

Second Row.—Slip 1, 1 plain, t over 1, 5 plain, t over 1, narrow, 7 plain, narrow, t over 1, 5 plain, t over 1, narrow, 7 plain, narrow, t over 1, 5 plain, t over 1, 2 plain.

Third Row.—Slip 1, 1 plain, t over 1, 1 plain, narrow, t over 1, 1 plain, t over 1, narrow, 1 plain, t over 1, narrow, 5 plain, narrow, t over 1, 1 plain, narrow, t over 1, 1 plain, t over 1, narrow, 1 plain, t over 1, narrow, 5 plain, narrow, t over 1, 1 plain, narrow, t over 1, 1 plain, t over 1, narrow, 1 plain, t over 1, 2 plain.

Fourth Row.—Slip 1, 1 plain, t over 1, 1 plain, narrow, t over 1, 3 plain, t over 1, narrow, 1 plain, t over 1, narrow, 3 plain, narrow, t over 1, 1 plain, narrow, t over 1, 3 plain, t over 1, narrow, 1 plain, t over 1, narrow, 3 plain, narrow, t over 1, 1 plain, narrow, t over 1, 3 plain, t over 1, narrow, 1 plain, t over 1, 2 plain.

Fifth Row.—Slip 1, 1 plain, t over 1, 1 plain, narrow, t over 1, 5 plain, t over 1, narrow, 1 plain, t over 1, narrow, 1 plain, narrow, t over 1, 1 plain, narrow, t over 1, 5 plain, t over 1, narrow, 1 plain, t over 1, narrow, 1 plain, narrow, t over 1, 1 plain, narrow, t over 1, 5 plain, t over 1, narrow, 1 plain, t over 1, 2 plain.

Sixth Row.—Slip 1, 1 plain, t over 1, 1 plain, narrow, t over 1, 3 plain, t over

1, narrow, 2 plain, t over 1, narrow, 1 plain, t over 1, narrow, 1 plain, pass narrowed stitch over plain stitch, t over 1, 1 plain, narrow, t over 1, 3 plain, t over 1, narrow, 2 plain, t over 1, narrow, 1 plain, t over 1, narrow, 1 plain, pass narrowed stitch over plain stitch, t over 1, 1 plain, narrow, t over 1, 3 plain, t over 1, narrow, 2 plain, t over 1, narrow, 1 plain, t over 1, 2 plain.

Seventh Row.—Slip 1, 1 plain, pass slipped stitch over plain one, 1 plain, t over 1, narrow, 1 plain, t over 1, narrow, 3 plain, narrow, t over 1, 1 plain, narrow, t over 1, 3 plain, t over 1, narrow, 1 plain, t over 1, narrow, 3 plain, narrow, t over 1, 1 plain, narrow, t over 1, 3 plain, t over 1, narrow, 1 plain, t over 1, narrow, 3 plain, narrow, t over 1, 1 plain, narrow, t over 1, 1 plain, narrow.

Eighth Row.—Slip 1, 1 plain, pass slipped stitch over plain stitch, 1 plain, t over 1, narrow, 1 plain, t over 1, narrow, 1 plain, narrow, t over 1, 1 plain, narrow, t over 1, 5 plain, t over 1, narrow, 1 plain, t over 1, narrow, 1 plain, narrow, t over 1, 1 plain, narrow, t over 1, 5 plain, t over 1, narrow, 1 plain, t over 1, narrow, 1 plain, narrow, t over 1, 1 plain, narrow, t over 1, 1 plain, narrow.

Ninth Row.—Slip 1, 1 plain, pass slipped stitch over plain one, 1 plain, t over 1, narrow, 1 plain, t over 1, narrow, 1 plain, pass narrowed stitch over plain stitch, t over 1, 1 plain, narrow, t over 1, 7 plain, t over 1, narrow, 1 plain, t over 1, narrow, 1 plain, pass narrowed stitch over plain 1, t over 1, 1 plain, narrow, t over 1, 7 plain t over 1, narrow, 1 plain, t over 1, narrow, 1 plain, pass narrow stitch over plain 1, t over 1, 1 plain, narrow, t over 1, 1 plain, narrow.

Tenth Row.—Slip 1, 1 plain, pass slipped stitch over plain stitch, 1 plain, t over 1, narrow, 3 plain, narrow, t over 1, 9 plain, t over 1, narrow, 3 plain, narrow, t over 1, 9 plain, t over 1, narrow, 3 plain, narrow, t over 1, 1 plain, narrow.

Eleventh Row.—Slip 1, 1 plain, pass slipped stitch over plain stitch, 1 plain, t over 1, narrow, 1 plain, narrow, t over 1, 11 plain, t over 1, narrow, 1 plain, narrow, t over 1, 11 plain, t over 1, narrow, 1 plain, narrow, t over 1, 1 plain, narrow.

Twelfth Row.—Slip 1, 1 plain, pass slipped stitch over plain stitch, 1 plain, t over 1, 3 together, t over 1, 13 plain, t over 1, 3 together, t over 1, 13 plain, t over 1, 3 together, t over 1, 1 plain, narrow.

Thirteenth Row.—Slip 1, 1 plain, pass slipped stitch over plain 1, 1 plain, t over 1, 1 plain, t over 1, narrow, 11 plain, narrow, t over 1, 1 plain, t over 1, narrow, 11 plain, narrow, t over 1, 1 plain, t over 1, 1 plain, narrow.

When first piece is long enough bind off loosely, then knit another piece same length and bind off loosely.

Embroidery.

The origin of embroidery is lost in antiquity, but it is known to have existed before painting, and to have been the first medium of reproducing natural objects in their natural colors.

The simplest form of embroidery is executed in outline work, and the stitch used is the simple stem stitch. A very popular article now used in embroidery is the linen flosses which come in beautiful shades, and repeated washing only improves the color. It is manufactured in Scotland and the sole agents for the United States are J. R. Leeson & Co., 298 Devonshire street, Boston, Mass. The flosses may be obtained at all retail stores.

A Pretty Tidy.

A Pretty Tidy. See description on page 60.

MATERIALS.—About two yards of robin-egg blue pongee. Decorate each end with a different design, as seen in cut. On one end have a light delicate vine which is executed in outline stitch using shades of linen floss, above described, to taste. Finish the other end with embroidered disks. Sew a pretty fringe on each end. When finished tie the scarf with a ribbon bow a little to one side of centre.

Embroidered Apron.   See description on page 61.

Embroidered Sunshade Cover.

If you have a good parasol frame, rip off the worn cover and cut out a new one by it. Pongee or sateen is pretty. Many use white. Cut the gores exactly by the old ones, and embroider each one separately. Scattered flowers are more used now than single bunches. Pansies, wild roses, clover, daisies, forget-me-nots, gold circles, an occasional dragon-fly or beetle, among the sprays, are all good designs. Do the work in outline, with the linen flosses, or, if you prefer, solidly.

Embroidered Apron.

This is made of plain white muslin. A strip of fine pongee is basted on, and this is first embroidered with any pretty design. Trim apron all round with a very fine knitted or crocheted lace of Finlayson, Bousfield & Co.'s REAL SCOTCH CROCHET THREAD. Black aprons are also very fashionable, and are pretty when embroidered with the linen flosses.

Pretty Design for Apron.

MATERIALS—Black Alpacca or sateen. Shades of Finlayson, Bousfield &

Co.'s linen flosses, designated below. The design may be put in the corner, or on bottom of apron. The pants of boy are worked in buff, the waist-coat blue, the coat brown, striped red and white stockings and cap. The plants are done in shades of green, and the railings brown. This design is also suitable for hand-bags, cushions, table scarfs, etc.

Embroidered Tidy for a Sofa.

Get very coarse hand-made linen, and cut the tidy 14½ inches wide, 1 yard 27½ inches long. The thick, straight edges, which go round the embroidery, are dark-blue linen floss; the triangles on the edge-border are alternately of

Work Apron.   For description see page 63.

blue and yellow, each with a centre of ecru color. All the stalks and foliage
are dark blue, while the flowers, blossoms and buds are edged with blue, filled
up with yellow, and have a centre of ecru; the latter color is repeated on the
dots of the stamens which are partly blue, partly ecru. The yellow filling of
the vase in the middle appears alternately plain and striped, as seen. Work
the peacocks with two rows of blue-stalk stitch; the crown, beak and legs are
entirely blue, the breast and neck have blue spots on a yellow satin-stitch
ground, these being smaller on the neck than on the breast. Work the feathers
of blue and ecru. The fringe is 3¾ inches long, made of strands of blue and
white linen floss, or a deep lace may be crocheted of REAL SCOTCH CRO-
CHET THREAD No. 50, and sewed on.

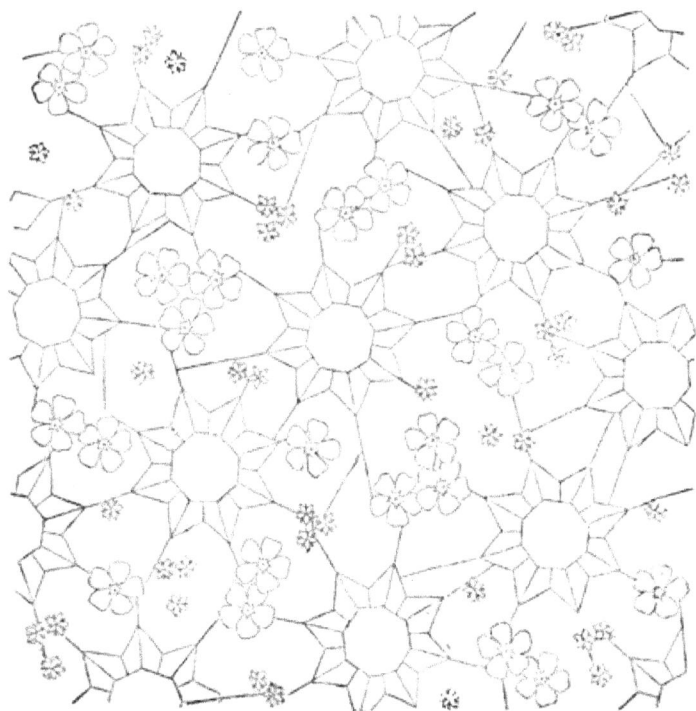

Design for Sofa Cushion.   For description see page 64.

A Work Apron.

MATERIALS—coarse linen outlined with the linen flosses before mentioned. The bottom part of apron is brought up and fastened forming a pocket. Trim apron all round with crocheted or knitted lace.

Design for Sofa Cushion.

Get black, or any shade, sateen, and embroider, in outline stitch, the design shown in different shades of the linen floss, or, if preferred, all one shade. Make up cushion as is usual. Trim all round with heavy cord and tassels.

Embroidered Table Scarf.

It will be easily seen from design how this scarf is put together. The material of the scarf is fine linen. The corner pieces are hemmed all round. Then take Java canvas and baste on the linen. Work a pretty cross-stitch design, with dark blue or red linen floss, used double. Then make a piece for centre of scarf. The canvas threads may be drawn out when finished, leaving the design on the linen. Put together with crocheted insertion and edge, or knitted of Finlayson, Bousfield & Co.'s REAL SCOTCH CROCHET THREAD. The first design in book would be pretty.

Felt Table Cover.

Get peacock or robin's egg blue felt. Baste canvas on wherever you intend to work a design. Then with dark yellow linen floss taken double work designs as seen in cut. When finished trim all round with pretty lace. It is quite the style to embroider lace with the shades of floss used in article.

Felt Table Cover.   For description see page 64.

Night-Dress Case.

Get a piece of linen 1 yard long and 12⅝ inches wide, lined with colored

silesia, is turned over 8⅝ inches at both ends and then sewn together so as to leave a pocket on each side, the two edges being ornamented with a most effective border worked into the stuff. A section of the border is shown. Use dark blue-linen floss for the embroidered stars used double. For the drawn

work squares draw out 16 threads in length and width leaving standing 8 threads. Leave outer edges by overcasting, using for drawn work white linen floss or blue. Crochet edge one blue one white scallop.

Embroidered Towel.

This linen towel is embroidered on both ends in some one of the many pretty cross stitch designs. Use blue or red linen floss and do cross-stitch over a piece of canvas the threads of which are afterwards drawn out.

Just above the fringe a narrow strip of drawn thread work is done.

Embroidered Towel. For description see page 66.

Sofa Cushion.

This is for common use. Make a pillow filled with feathers and covered with colored silesia. Then get the openwork scrim which can be bought cheaply and on the plain stripes with linen flosses embroider some pretty design. The cushion may be covered both sides with the scrim and finished off at 4 corners with bows of ribbon.

Sofa Cushion.   For description see page 67.

A Pretty Pen-Wiper.

Take for the top of the pen-wiper a piece of embroidered felt. The embroidery is done with shaded linen flosses. Under the top piece have three or four plain pieces of felt pinked. The edge of embroidered piece is finished with a heavy gilt cord. Put a crescent ornament of gilt in the centre.

Embroidered Doilies.

These doilies are of congress canvas embroidered in cross stitch with linen flosses of blue or red shade; the canvas is cut an inch and a half longer each

way than is needed for the doily, and the edges are fringed out 1½ inches. They are all worked differently.   Any pretty cross stitch designs will do.

Embroidered Tobacco Bag.

The bag is of olive sateen or pongee, ornamented with figures worked in outline with red linen floss.   Work a monogram above the figures on front side. The edge is cut in scallops, and is buttonholed round top with red linen floss. The lower edge is drawn together and finished with a tassel.   The bag is 5½ inches deep and 7 inches wide; it is lined with wash-leather or oil-silk.   It has a slide about 1½ inches from the top, with silk cord to draw it up and is finished with tassels.

Richelieu Guipure.

This is work of a modern date, and differs but little from Roman, Strasbourg, and Venetian Embroidery.   It is founded upon the ancient Point Coupé, or Cutwork, which was one of the first laces, and was extensively used in conjunction with Linen Embroidery on the Continent and in England from the fourteenth to the sixteenth centuries, when it was superseded by Reticella Lace.   The modern Richelieu Guipure differs from the old Cutwork in being worked in more open patterns, and separated by Bars formed of threads Buttonholed over.   In the old work the linen foundations were cut and Buttonholed over wherever Bars were required, and the patterns were closer and more solid, almost entirely covered with needlework, and required greater patience and skill in their execution.

For many varieties of trimmings and for washing materials, Richelieu Guipure is well adapted, for, as long as the foundation is selected of good strong stuff, there is no reason why the Embroidery should not be as lasting as the old Point Coupé, specimens of which, worked in the fifteenth century, are still to be seen. To work, select cream white, pure white, or écru colored linen, or cotton foundation, upon which trace the outline of the pattern and indicate the lines for the Bars. Back this foundation with brown paper should it not be stiff, but this is not generally necessary. Then RUN all the outlines with a double line of thread or silk, using a color matching the material; Run the second line of thread the sixteenth of an inch above the first, and work the Bars during the process of Running. These make thus: Throw two threads across the space the Bar is to cover, catch them well into the edges of the pattern, and then BUTTONHOLE them thickly over, and make a PICOT in the centre Bar. Then carefully Buttonhole over every outline with the same colored silk or thread; always turn the edge of the Buttonhole to the side of the material that is to be afterwards cut away. Great nicety is required to keep so many lines of Buttonhole all of the same width and thickness, and the second Running of each line will here prove very useful, as, if the needle be always put in just beyond it, the width of each line will be the same. The thickness will depend upon the perfect regularity of distance with which each stitch is taken after the preceding one.   This Embroidery is done with Finlayson, Bousfield & Co.'s linen floss. The usual practice is to match the color of foundation, but red, blue, and black linen floss make pretty borders to écru or drab-colored linens.

If the work is intended for a trimming to a mantel board, one edge of it will be made straight where it is sewn on, and the other scalloped. This scalloped edge must be ornamented with Picots, like those made upon the Bars. Having finished all the Buttonholing, proceed to cut away the foundation material from under the Bars. Use sharp and small scissors, and cut very slowly from underneath the Bars and not over them. The Bars are much stronger and neater when made during the progress of Running than if worked when the material is cut away (as is sometimes recommended), but the cutting out of the superfluous stuff is rendered much more troublesome by their presence.

This work requires a background to throw it in relief, although it can be worked as an edging to table-cloths, and will then not require one. A colored cloth is the most suitable one for mantel borders, but satin or velvet look rich when Richelieu Guipure is used for cushions or banner screens.

INDEX.

Crocheting.

Knitting.

Embroidery.

www.ingramcontent.com/pod-product-compliance
Lightning Source LLC
Chambersburg PA
CBHW022145090426
42742CB00010B/1395